CW00500935

Writers of Wales

———————————————

Editors
MEIC STEPHENS   R. BRINLEY JONES

Donald Evans

RHYDWEN WILLIAMS

University of Wales Press

Cardiff 1991

I

Rhydwen Williams is a Rhondda poet. This explains why he has done more than anyone else to safeguard the coal-miner's epic in Welsh literature. It accounts too for his tendency to look at Wales and the world in general with the spirit of a collier's son. He has written on all the major issues of life in the twentieth century from this tenacious and compassionate standpoint. As he himself once remarked: *I always view life from the top of Moel Cadwgan*. His work is an expression of the powerful genesis of his identity, the formation of a sympathetic and rebellious soul.

All of his immediate forbears, on his mother's side, came from north Wales to Pentre in the Rhondda Fawr in 1900, forced to leave their native Dyffryn Nantlle owing to the death of the father, Robert Williams. Robert Williams had combined quarrying and his Noncomformist ministry as minister of Nasareth and Pantglas Independent Chapels, Llanllyfni. Rhydwen's grandparents on his father's side were farming folk, earning their living on a two-acred smallholding, Gelli, near Holywell in Flintshire, until hardship compelled them to move to south Wales in search of a better standard of living.

At that time, the Rhondda with its booming steam-coal industry was luring people, not only from all over Wales, but also from the south-western counties of England, and even as far afield as Scotland and Ireland. Lead miners and quarrymen flocked there from north Wales during the first decade of the twentieth century.

Between 1880 and 1911 the Rhondda experienced a massive increase in population, and industrial expansion turned a wooded and pastoral land into what Dr E. D. Lewis has appropriately called *a vast black Klondike*. It was here, in this confined valley, that crowds of immigrants, the Welsh being by far in the majority, hurled themselves together in order to dig a livelihood from a fierce subterranean world, and in the process managed to grow into a unique society of working-class people.

Rhydwen's first major prose work, the trilogy of novels, CWM HIRAETH, traces the part which his own family played, through the upheavals and vicissitudes of a three-generation span, in the formation of such a community. In these novels his family's lives are shown to be closely entwined with the intense changes and critical movements of the period and as such give the entire story the atmosphere of a creative social document. Indeed, Kate Roberts criticized Rhydwen Williams for largely ignoring the essential relationships and internal conflicts between his kin in everyday life, the indispensable ingredients of any worthwhile novel. However, in this case, one would be justified in regarding such an observation as a misinterpretation of the writer's intention, for his primary concern was to chronicle and illustrate his family's participation in the miners' struggle against the coal owners for a decent working life and a fair wage, rather than to concentrate on revealing their personal disagreements with each other. By adopting this approach he was fiercely reliving some of the moulding forces of his own childhood. CWM HIRAETH is a family biography.

The first novel, Y BRIODAS *(The Wedding)*, deals with life in the Rhondda from 1900 to 1915 when the area was a cauldron of discontent. The poignancy of the strike is shown by the inner compulsion which forced Rhydwen's uncle, a refined poet and thinker, Uncle Siôn, Lleteca, to become a Socialist rebel and an inciter of mass meetings. By embracing the new ideals, he is shown to have clashed bitterly with the old Nonconformist values of his family and acquaintances. Many of the young aggressive leaders of the coalfields had once been prominent contributors to chapel life: Noah Ablett, for example, was a former Sunday-school teacher, while A. J. Cook and Arthur Horner served as lay preachers. Uncle Siôn's smouldering disillusionment with a meek and submissive tradition became militant at the funeral service of Ben Bowen, the young Rhondda poet who died of tuberculosis, the disease which had already killed many other young people and was a result of the degrading living conditions in the valley:

The Sunday, puritanical smells came to his nostrils from the pine. Seeing so many people sitting so solemn and quiet in the varnished seats frightened him. Man is so docile! So powerless! The huge organ and the pulpit possessed some grandeur, and the gold letters on the wall were beautiful, but . . . was there a solution in this fearful, wailing, helpless congregation to the anxieties, oppressions and tragedies of man? . . . Perhaps all Noncomformity would do was to listen passively amongst the clamour of pain and deaths, groaning and lamenting, and sing a hymn as if that were a contribution to life's calamity in a dump like this.

Siôn resolved his quandary by opting to throw in his lot with the rebels' political strategy for alleviating the misery of the coal-mining fraternity. He became distrustful of Mabon (William Abraham), the pious mediator between the colliers and the employers, and the first president of the South Wales Miners' Federation. The Sunday-school arguments became meaningless and foolish; it was hardly the time for anachronistic theological discussions:

I know that the Epistle to the Hebrews, whether written by Paul, Barnabas or Simon the Magician, is not so vital as securing fair and proper hours for a labourer to claw coal in the depths of the earth.

In such an atmosphere of contention even Evan Roberts's Revival which blazed through the Rhondda in 1905 and 1906 had no impact on Siôn, although his mother was an ardent follower of all its meetings.

The South Wales Miners' Federation was founded in 1898. This soon became part of the Miners' Federation of Great Britain. In 1900 a new Labour Party emerged in south Wales with the election of Keir Hardie as the Member of Parliament for Merthyr. The miners challenged the sliding scale system by which wages fluctuated according to the unsteady price of coal. They also called for an eight-hour working shift, and in 1909 the Eight Hour Act was passed. Continued dispute led to the Minimum Wage Act of 1912 which awarded to the miner a minimum wage of around four shillings and sixpence a day. Unrest, however, did not abate. The younger protagonists pressed not only for more privileges but even advocated a policy to decrease production in order to destroy the employers. They published these new ideals in a hostile pamphlet, *The Miners' Next Step.*

But far underneath these benefits, necessary as they were, the dark tunnels and caves, the subconscious of the whole community, and the source of all its anguish, remained as deadly as ever. It is hardly surprising that some of Rhydwen's strongest passages are those where he is reporting back from the exact point of contact between the workers and the incessant dangers of their daily grind. His portrayals of the Rhondda environment are vigorous and trenchant. Time and time again they are expressed by the means of a moving and dynamic rhetoric:

No one can comprehend what darkness is till his eyes stare at the earth's intestines; for that matter, no one can understand what silence is until his ears listen to the primordial forests which slumber layer upon layer beneath the huge mountains. Neither the stars nor the moon nor the expanses above, more than the surrounding summits, slopes and plains, can offer exactly the same thrill as that which a man feels when treading for the first time along the black, unbelievable, unforeseen, unending kingdom of the surly entrails of the earth. The caverns have eyes. The silence can follow him like quarrelsome dogs, barking and biting at his heels. It is true that a map of every section is kept in every office above the pit, and that the measurements of every heading and coal-face are down on paper as a guideline for the miner; yet, every worker who ventures there daily with his pickaxe and shovel knows that he is faced by an occasional corner and turning that no map can forewarn him against, and a few crises and perils which nobody can foresee or measure their length and breadth. The chill at the pit's entrance can freeze a man to the bone. The heat in the far recesses of the mine can suffocate like a scorched wilderness. The glistening coal whispers. Hollow after hollow echoes it. The knotty trees curse and blaspheme the mountain's weight. The rope from the double-parting to the road-gate moans all the way. The gas can be felt from afar like rotten breath. Even an old drowsy simple post waits for a chance to be awkward.

The second novel, Y SIÔL WEN (*The White Shawl*), begins in the same forceful vein with a stirring description of living conditions in the valley. The year is 1916, the year of Rhydwen's birth. (He was born on 29 August, and christened Robert Rhydwenfro, Robert in honour of his maternal grandfather and Rhydwenfro in honour of his paternal grandfather's eldest brother who also distinguished himself in the Nonconformist pulpit.) The section is an account of the stormy weather which coincided with the hour of his birth. The reader finds himself trapped in an upstairs room of a collier's dwelling in Pentre with the expectant mother, sharing her anxiety as she watches the swollen river rising menacingly and the wind pounding the mountains and the hanging coal tips. Scenes of this nature convey the physical intensity of the Rhondda and the durability of its inhabitants.

But despite the hardships, Rhydwen's childhood was a health-gaining time of forming natural roots and sprouting a joyful sense of wholeheartedly belonging to the people and soil of his valley. He had a cultured upbringing in a cosy God-worshipping home. His father was an excellent provider and his mother an accomplished and principled guardian who used to read to him from the novels of Daniel Owen, thus giving her son a definite and solid Welsh literary consciousness. His Uncle Siôn kindled in him a love for Welsh poetry, his uncle Robert Owen was also a lover of words and another uncle, John David, was a skilled artist with oils. Furthermore, the Baptist Chapel of Moriah, under the leadership of its minister, Robert Griffith, was an invaluable nurturing influence. Here, regular communal activities such as drama renderings, choir performances and penny readings were held, and the preacher's powerfully delivered sermons had a far-reaching impact. Rhydwen's school career, particularly in its later stages, apart from the inspiring lessons of one teacher, the erudite Mr Lee, was rather a stifling experience serving only to test endurance and prod rebellion, but the fauna and flora of Moel Cadwgan were constant compensatory attractions, enriching him with a scrupulous sensitivity for the delights of nature and the beginning of a life-long love of birds and animals.

But the tribulations of the coalfield were never far away. The drop in demand for coal after the First World War was to bring fresh afflictions to the Rhondda. It ushered in the long meagre years of the depression and the enraged encounters between the miners and the law-enforcing bodies of the authorities — the police and the army. These were the years which piled extra worries on the shoulders of Rhydwen's father who was already familiar with the horrors of the battlefield as well as with pit disasters and employers' conspiracies:

Dreaming is easy for a growing child . . .

Thomas's world was one of facts. Facts as obvious, monotonous and black as the big surrounding tips. It was a good world when there were not enough wagons to contain the coal more than hours to cut it . . . his father alive . . . his family around him. Now the war years (and preceding years) had destroyed the foundations of the industry, the Rhondda's best seams had been mercilessly depleted in order to bring sudden prosperity to the privileged, the price of coal was low on the market and the miner's life full of shadows, doubts and fears. He had been unemployed for months. Naturally, he had not been idle. He had two big gardens on the side of Pen-twyn Mountain. It had been a glorious summer and the sun and soil had blessed him. But . . . by now he was a father of four. The kind earth could yield a sack of potatoes and saucepans of peas and beans, but . . . money in the purse was a

7

necessity to buy boots and clothe children. He had no idea when he was going to work again. He had been scratching for coal, on his knees by candlelight, from the level with Siôn, and they managed to get enough to keep the grate alight. At times, he would be very depressed about the future, what his responsibility should be, because Rhondda's population relied entirely on the pits. There was no future between the mountains any more.

After the year 1924, in which there was a short rise in coal production, and especially following the strike of 1926, the coal industry of the Rhondda showed a sharp decline. This was due to the loss of markets following the Versailles treaty and the growth of hydro-electric power abroad, but mainly to the substitution of oil for coal by the mercantile marine and navy. In a land so overwhelmingly dependent on one industry this led to a cessation of output, unemployment and poverty. Now the influx of population which the valley had witnessed at the outset of the century began ironically to turn into a mass exodus. During the twenties nearly two and a half million people moved from south Wales to the Midlands and south-eastern England in search of employment. Rhydwen's family joined the throng of emigrants. They left the Rhondda in 1931 for Christleton in Cheshire where his father had secured a job as an insurance agent. Y SIÔL WEN closes with a description of the removal lorry slowly moving out of Pentre and the sight of Moel Cadwgan and Pwll-y-bedw on its journey towards England. This rent was to lacerate him internally to such an extent that the scars remain red and raw to the present day.

Indeed, this particular pain is the central theme of the third novel, DYDDIAU DYN *(The Days of Man)*. It is a book steeped in a profound and unrelieved *hiraeth;* the song of a young exile during the lean 1930s languishing in an English city and longing for his Welsh mining valley. There was a vicious circle of aggravations and inducements in every facet of his new home and of city life in general, all contributing towards the sharpening of his ever simmering feelings into stabs of agony:

And the imagination began to work in my head and the hiraeth in my abdomen, and I was back once again in Cwm Rhondda, climbing Moel Cadwgan, standing with the boys by the opening of a level, venturing, walking in the dark, and the dampness beginning to itch the nostrils, and the moisture down the sides starting to tickle the ears . . . I ran in panic back to the kitchen. I felt without a doubt that something very big had happened to me as I stood as empty and abandoned as a milk bucket on a yard waiting for the herd, the calamity which my mother always feared when she used to warn me `not to get lost'; it had happened at last, much worse than being lost on Pen-twyn mountain or Moel Cadwgan or Barry Island's golden beaches, because I was still in the presence of my family, safely under the roof of my new home, but I was lost . . . lost . . . lost in the great wide world outside Cwm Rhondda and Wales. And there was an anxiety within me as if I were sensing with a sorcerer's insight that I would remain lost for the rest of my life . . . Oh, I wish I could decide whether I was sane or not!

Soon the Welsh chapel at Chester, Penri Memorial, began to prove irksome. Religion had become unfamiliar. The act of praising God was not enjoyable any more. The old hymns sounded stereotyped and the sermons threadbare. The Welshness of the congregation was a veneer and their whole manner and behaviour a striving to maintain appearance and preserve privilege rather than taking part in a genuine act of worship.

The scowling English populace was another factor of offence. Rhydwen could sense their unmistakable aloofness and even enmity every time he stepped out of doors. He was bitterly assured of his intuition by the hostile reception he received at the local secondary school. He found the attitude and behaviour of its staff and pupils alike so antagonistic that he left the place after only a single disastrous day's attendance. But this brought him no joy. His first employment as a gardener's mate was even more painful. The exceptional crudity and vehemence of the head gardener caused him at times to wish that he was back in the school which he renounced so eagerly. The episode instilled in him a life-long hatred of any commanding imperious person in authority.

Before long his *hiraeth* was forged into a double-edged sword. Not only did events in Chester serve to remind him often of the Rhondda, but the Rhondda itself began to frequent his home in Cheshire in the pitiful form of his Uncle Siôn who brought news of the oppression, unemployment and hunger which were still ravaging the valleys. The sight of this gentle cultured man having been reduced by the Macdonald and the National Government into haggard flesh and bleeding feet not only symbolized the fragmentation of life in the Rhondda but the suffering of the underprivileged everywhere on earth:

It was a hell of a thing to oppress people and transplant them here and yonder, move families from one environment to another, changing language, changing neighbours, changing society . . . And a hell of a thing to turn a man like Uncle Siôn into a vagrant over the face of the earth, his own soil, the mountains of Wales, the hills of the Cwm, a tramp on his own land as if nothing belonged to him in this world any more except a belly . . . stomach . . . and his bright, musical, beautiful, kind intellect as empty as the head of every dumb animal whose dung I had to clear every awful morning.

10

*The colours and shapes of sadness were a solace for me. I could
see in them one basic fact which kept me from splintering apart
at sixteen years of age; the fact that the pale suffering in my
mother's face and the red anger in my father's countenance and
the terror which floored me so frequently were not entirely pri-
vate, special and personal to us. This was the pain which was part
and parcel of the human heart. The affliction and crisis which
were inseparable from the face of mankind.*

In Chester the presence, temperament and influence
of the author's mother came to fulfil a far-reaching
role. In the preceding novels her strength and personality and depth of convictions regarding religious
matters and Welsh-language issues had been warmly
and faithfully recorded, but here she grew to person-
ify the most fundamental meanings of the uprooting
of a whole community from the Rhondda's soil. Under
her guidance, the hearth and the home develops into
an island of warmth and Welshness amongst an alien
sea. Suddenly she emerges as the heroine of the trilogy, becoming almost an object of worship to her son
— a mother of pure love with gentle labouring hands,
the fountain-head of his Welsh essence, the rock of his
existence: a woman of everlasting hiraeth for the
Rhondda, perpetually facing her life's pitiless fate
with a dignified resignation:

*. . . and she loved with a sincerity that nobody possesses except
the soul who has conquered the world. The kind of love, were it
not victorious, that would shatter the heart to shivers.*

She typifies a basic human goodness, as well as the
undying spirit of Rhondda, and the last testimony of
the final novel, at her burial time, links up artistically
with the tribute at the beginning of the first:

And yet, yet I know that she is still around these eloquent mountains, from nook to rock, from summit to field, from well to waterfall, from stream to forest, from neighbourhood to hearthstone, and in her face, name and beauty I shall see the mounds and tips and these raw miles worthy to be acknowledged as part of the 'vineyard given to us'.

II

From 1931, when he was fifteen years old, until his fiftieth birthday in 1966, with the exception of a six-year interval when he worked for a television company, the call to minister directed the course of Rhydwen Williams's life. According to his testimonies in GORWELION *(Horizons)*, an autobiography published in 1984, the craft of preaching became a thrilling enticement for him during his adolescent years. The sonorous seeds sown by Robert Griffith from Moriah's pulpit, and the germ of excitement which he himself had felt in that same pulpit during his early singing and reciting exploits were germinating into an ambition for a ministerial vocation. He began to take note of the vocal quality of individual preachers, and the unique style with which each one delivered his sermons. At this time he was an avid frequenter of preaching meetings. Many of the well-known preachers of the period, men like Jubilee Young and Glasnant Young, left an indelible impression on the youngster during their eloquent visits to north Wales. Rhydwen became a shop assistant at Colwyn Bay, and his zeal for preaching was so fervent that he even snatched time to practise various techniques of delivery amongst the cats and the flour of the warehouse. (During the phase covered by this chapter, he also worked in a post office, an insurance office, a factory, an inn and on the railroad.) Even at that early stage he had formulated a definite philosophy concerning the most effective mode of preaching. It was as essential for a sermon to contain flights of rhetoric and imagination as sincerity of content. Preaching was an art

and its most able exponents were polished performers, majestic orators. It is no wonder that Saunders
Lewis regarded Rhydwen as one of the richest voices
reading poetry on radio and television.

Another major influence on his mental growth during
these years was the burning of the Bombing School at
Penyberth by Lewis Valentine, D. J. Williams and
Saunders Lewis. In 1936 Rhydwen became a Welsh
Nationalist of conviction. In his case that step was much
more than an adoption of a new political creed, in fact
it was an acquisition of a distinct spiritual direction
amidst the conflicting dogmas of the time —
Fundamentalism and Communism. The events of 1936
fell on receptive ground which had been well tilled
through the formative years in the Rhondda by his
mother and his Uncle Siôn:

... despite my eagerness to enter the ministry, the mark of some
sort of piety (as I thought) which was attached to this made me ill
at ease, if that is the word; not that I yearned to live prodigally and
uncontrollably nor was likely to do so, but the conception of behav-
ing and talking in a godly guise after the manner of the City Mission
folk was quite incompatible with my nature, although I had the
greatest respect for them. By becoming a Welsh Nationalist I was
sensing the history and tradition of the little nation to which I
belonged, and the Christian ministry took on a whole new mean-
ing ... More than that, I perceived that writing poetry was not just
a hobby or a pleasure for a mere emotional creature, but had been
from the beginning a Christian vocation in Wales with a much
older tradition than either Chaucer or Shakespeare in England ...
and in addition to that the Christian viewpoint essentially included
a strong respect for nationhood.

These were difficult years for Rhydwen,' a time of
unceasing struggle to secure an adequate education
to prepare himself for and to survive under bleak eco-

nomic conditions, and a period of unrelenting friction, often self-inflicted he confesses, with his denominational establishment. Firstly, he enlisted as a student in a preparatory school in Swansea, but his stay there turned out to be a short and unhappy one. On leaving Ilston, he was invited to attend classes held by John Powell Griffiths in his home at Rhosllannerchrugog. Here, as in Swansea, the overwhelming attraction which writing prose and poetry held for him proved distracting, much to the annoyance of his teacher. However, under Powell Griffiths's tuition he passed the entrance examination of Carmarthen College which afforded him admission to a twelve-month course at the University College of Swansea.

On his second stay at Swansea, the relationship between him and his denomination became exceptionally tense. His reluctance to follow a specified Hebrew course at the expense of abandoning his Welsh studies was the basic cause. Also, a burning interest in the theatre was another diversion, and he became more and more influenced by the heady spirit of his times: books like BRAVE NEW WORLD by Aldous Huxley, held an exciting attraction for him; the Spanish Civil War was in progress and he was captivated by the great political statements made by contemporary writers like Auden, Spender and Orwell in England and the poetry of Aneirin Talfan Davies and W. H. Reese in Wales; new and agitating impressions reflected in unconventional sermons at frequent Sunday engagements at the time, and his open rebelliousness:

Neither the chapel nor the denomination nor the ministry of my ambition resembled any more what I thought at first. It was a narrow respectable world of superficial values, middle-class super-

stitions, nurturing artificial godliness, with little interest in literature, art and the theatre, the things which civilize people. And what real interest was there by a denomination in a paltry student, for that matter, unless he possessed exceptional academic potential and the conventional marks of his fold.

As a result of this uncompromising attitude he was summoned in front of the senate, and they categorically showed their disapproval of his unorthodoxy. Hitler's dictatorial policies in Europe soon led to the outbreak of the Second World War, and Rhydwen's application for an exemption from military service as a theological student was refused. They said that a spell of discipline would be of benefit to the young man. Although forced to leave Swansea, a new academic session saw him as a student in the University College of North Wales at Bangor, defiantly passing his Welsh studies, but thin finances and a second order to enlist quickly terminated his ambitions. During the following months he was on the run as a conscientious objector, moving warily from place to place, sleeping rough and living by his wits. He joined a Quaker ambulance team and witnessed the carnage German bombers inflicted on Liverpool, an experience realistically narrated in the last chapter of GORWELION.

However, in 1941 the climate seemed to change. Ainon, Ynys-hir, one of the churches willing to turn a blind eye to rigid denominational requirements, welcomed him. Naturally, he grabbed the opportunity. Ainon, renowned, linked with the memorable R. B. Jones, was also an uncompromising fortress of Fundamentalism. The young minister was soon up against it again, sometimes to the point of despair. However, when the clouds were darkest above him, it was at Ynys-hir that he came into contact with

Kitchener and Mair Davies, introduced by the extraordinary and saintly George M. Ll. Davies, whom he met at the home of Margaret Davies who set about changing things for him and urging him to fulfil himself as a poet and a writer.

During the war years, the Cadwgan group of poets and writers became prominent. Cadwgan, home of J. Gwyn Griffiths and his wife Kate Bosse-Griffiths, on the slopes of Moel Cadwgan, was the refuge for a small gathering of kindred souls who met for political, religious and literary discussions. Besides the two already mentioned, the cluster contained nine regular members: D. R. Griffiths and Gwilym Griffiths (J. Gwyn Griffiths's brothers), Pennar Davies, Rosemarie Wolff (who later became Mrs Pennar Davies), Gareth Alban Davies, John Hughes, William Thomas, T. Vaughan Lewis and Rhydwen Williams. In BARDDAS (February 1982) Rhydwen describes Cadwgan as a shelter from the wind and a fort when the world was on fire. The activities, discussions and stimulating intellectual atmosphere within the Cadwgan circle have been thoroughly illustrated in his novel ADAR Y GWANWYN *(Birds of Spring)*. Indeed, the book may be regarded as a kind of portrayal of three of its most prominent members, J. Gwyn Griffiths, his wife and Pennar Davies, as well as an unequivocal criticism of the barbarity, hysteria and conventionalism which prevailed in Welsh religion and politics in the forties:

Life is not easy for any one of us now. At a time like this, the shadow of war everywhere, a close community is not expected to welcome rascals like us. Conscientious objectors! Heretics! Traitors! Chapel to chapel, tavern to tavern, home to home, how many friends have we from one end of the valley to the other. They are rare, my boy, they are rare. This is why we must stick together. Loyalty is fundamental. Paramount. At the present time.

The novel also reveals the alternative values of the Cadwgan group regarding literature. They stressed the freedom of the writer to deal with any aspect of life in a more realistic manner than had been hitherto done in Wales. Also, the moral responsibilities of the artist were crucial: it was of the uttermost importance for him to reflect personal experience, solid belief and firm principles in a precise cause. The Cadwgan writers were unusually bold, challenging the customary standards of the religious establishments. Some of their published work incited objection from the traditionalists, like Rhydwen's daring short story, 'Lludw i'r Lludw' *(Dust to Dust)*, for example, when it appeared in the magazine Y FFLAM in 1947. Reviewed in one Welsh newspaper, one of the most eminent of Noncomformist leaders scorned such writing and dismissed the author as a sex maniac. But according to Rhydwen it was a tender love-story, true every word, of a young soldier killed in France who left his sweetheart behind, pregnant; a story illustrating the frustrated life and death of a bold-minded sensual youth in an ordinary puritanical society. As he wrote in ADAR Y GWANWYN:

Well, we are a society underneath this roof, and producing literature — poetry, stories, novels, hymns — is a means of extracting a new consciousness from our sense of nationhood and faith.

The group advocated a break from the old sweet eisteddfodic lyricism of the past, and the plaintive odes of the strict-metre poets. Literature had to be full of thoughts and ideas. This probably accounts for the factual nature of most of Rhydwen's novels. In 1953 a selection of the group's poetry was published under the title CERDDI CADWGAN. It is of a wide and varied nature, ranging from the experimental and contemplative through the sarcastic, learned and the sensuous to the patriotic and the international — a true reflection of their broad unconventional convictions. In the introduction each poet gives his views on the place of propaganda, traditional forms, obscurity and birds and flowers in poetry. Here are Rhydwen's opinions on the four topics:

It is unavoidable in responsible poetry. A poet is a normal being. Poetry is not a form of his neurosis. A church suits him better than a clinic, a crusade than a club. Only a waxwork image can be neutral — many of those write poetry! Responsibility is the difference between a poet and a boar. Propaganda and great literature may coexist; e.g. the Sermon on the Mount.

I am fond of traditional poetry; I like every kind of poetry. And I believe that all true poetry is disciplined. It is maintained that free poetry is not poetry at all. I think it is, but it is not free. There are more than twenty-four metres to it. I regard the traditional metres a blessing and a curse. It was they which gave splendour to our literature. The splendour of Dafydd ap; the decadence of ap Dafydd.

I oppose obscurity in poetry.

A welcome to them! God included them in creation. Who am I to refuse then in a song? I have heard the saying that the lowest of men is more valuable than a field of flowers and a heaven full of birds. Chesterton wrote about the donkey, but he chose the most dignified donkey in history before managing to extract poetry from it.

III

In 1946 Rhydwen Williams moved from Ynys-hir to Resolfen. During that August he was proclaimed the Crown poet at the Mountain Ash National Eisteddfod. This must have been a very satisfying achievement, making amends for the obscurity, rejections and disappointments of the preceding years. Moreover, the winning poem, the distillation of all of Rhydwen's unconventional feelings, thoughts and faith up to that juncture, is also most noteworthy.

A choice of two subjects was given that year, 'Yr Arloeswr' *(The Pioneer)* and 'Preiddiau Annwn' *(The Hounds of the Underworld)*. Twenty-three poets submitted entries, and the competition turned out to be one of high standard with four worthy of the Crown. The three adjudicators, T. J. Morgan, J. M. Edwards and William Morris, were unanimous in their decision in favour of Rhydwen's *pryddest*. Furthermore, they were all generous with praise. They emphasized the daring, confidence and novelty of the winning poet; in the words of T. J. Morgan, *his vocabulary ventures over the nest of tradition in order to reach terms and figures to express his modern ideas.* The poem, embellished by frequent alliteration and strengthened by double rhyming, was written in long flowing sonnets with twelve to fifteen syllables in each line, the metre which R. Williams Parry used to construct his new sonnets in the second part of the thirties, and Caradog Prichard adopted to write his well-known *pryddest* on suicide, 'Terfysgoedd Daear' *(The World's Commotions)*, for the Denbigh National Eisteddfod, 1939. At the time 'Yr Arloeswr' was hailed as a new work in the field of the Crown poems, a composition of fresh, tough and contemporary style. In fact it was exactly this feature which gave it the decisive edge over the second best, and excellent traditional lyrical *pryddest* by Dafydd Jones, Ffair-rhos, dealing with a smallholder's struggle to pioneer a difficult stretch of land.

God is the pioneer of Rhydwen's poem. In the first part He reconsiders the act of Creation. After the first stirring of His visions over the void, the stars were pinned on the night's canvas, the mist swirled on its journey, and the mountains moulded within their boundaries. Conception and birth followed, and all forms of life, crows as well as kings, ceaselessly began to enter the world through the same pathway. As T. J. Morgan significantly remarked, *the flow of the poem is that the Holy Spirit decides to create Life and the Universe, and this creation is a combination of an orthodox process and the scientific interpretation:*

> *Codais y cripil i'w lys o laid yr iselder —*
> *di-wrid o flaen engyl, di-fost o flaen bregus bryf!*
> *Gwisgwyd ei noethni â hugan lân f'aruchelder —*
> *cynddelw duw doeth o sylwedd epaod cryf; —*
> *a'i ado'n denant direidus cread cyfannedd,*
> *cyn pondro a droid duwdod ryw ddydd o'i annedd.*

(I lifted the cripple to his court from the mud of the deep— shameless in front of angels, boastless before a frail fly! His nakedness was dressed with the pure garment of my majesty — the archetype of a wise god from the substance of powerful apes; — and left him a mischievous tenant of a habitable creation, before pondering whether deity would be expelled one day from his dwelling.)

In the second section the Pioneer declares His complete satisfaction, after ages of evolution and experiment, with the faultless nature of His Son, *Earth's hanged bastard, the King of heaven!* Again T. J. Morgan's remarks are interesting: *I do not know what the orthodox would say about the style, it is at the best of times short on religious reverence.* The imagery is original. The Saviour is described as the perfect copy emerging from the press of the Incarnation. God had continuously listened through His merciful radio to *the drunken performers on the furious wavelengths of the flesh.* He had constantly tried to broadcast His beseeching programmes, but man had always smashed the corporation's gear, thereby deafening generation after generation. Man had also hired the devil's orchestra; the show was being produced by Death and even the angels of heaven had been bribed to sing in his choir. But through all the desecrating, the Pioneer had in His Son a miraculous source of joy: *a highway of goodness through the labyrinth of evil; music of an immortal world from Calvary's silence*:

> Marwolaeth yw eithaf celwydd, tric rhith cyn diflannu;
> gwisg-ôd y Gwirionedd yw bywyd, y pannwr a'r pannu!

(Death is the extremity of deceit, an illusion trick before vanishing; the snowy garment of the Truth is life, the fuller and the fulling!)

In the third part, God's wrath is incited by man's wilful interference with the atom. He forewarns him of the terrible consequences of such foolish meddling; the torn earth would resemble a nightmarish burial ground with vultures preying on the carcases:

> Er chwarae ohonot â'r mellt heb losgi dy fysedd,
> disgyblaf â gronyn anorthrech dy gabl a'th rysedd.

(Although you play with lightning without burning your fingers,
I will discipline your blasphemy and excesses with an uncon-
querable particle.)

But even when humans are only a memory and *all the curtains ablaze*, the Pioneer would still continue to keep *His right on creation's temple* on which He would perform His most unbelievable act of all: ensuring that mortals would survive forever. Death would be destroyed and the grave buried, the fulfilment of His plan:

Bydd Amser, gwas bach yr ystad, yn rhoi'i gryman i'r ddaear
i rydu dros byth ar ôl torri'r canrifoedd ir . . .
Caf orffwys yn dawel mewn byd na fedd ond dechreuad,
myfi, yr arloeswr, mor dawel â'r dyn yn y lleuad!

(Time, the estate petty labourer, will put away his sickle
to rust forever after cutting the green centuries . . .
I can rest quietly in a world that has only a beginning,
myself, the pioneer, as quiet as the man in the moon!)

The year following the Eisteddfod at Mountain Ash, Rhydwen left Resolfen to become the minister at Carmel, Pontlliw. He served there until 1959. These were years of contentment: he was working amongst a total Welsh community; his congregation overfilling the chapel every Sunday; he himself adjudicating frequently in local eisteddfodau (he recalls giving the first prize to Siân Phillips for recitation in an eisteddfod at Clydach), and writing plays for chapel and village functions. But these are not to be regarded as a serious part of Rhydwen's literary repertoire. Indeed, he himself dismisses them, and rightly so, as occasional exercises for public use. But what they do signify, however, in conjunction with his other involvements is that the Pontlliw period was an industrious and a rewarding phase of his life.

In 1959 he moved to Rhyl on the north Wales coast. It is most unlikely that he would have uprooted himself from the warm and friendly environment of Pontlliw in the Swansea valley. However, journeying north to visit his parents, Rhydwen met with a serious motor accident which meant him being hospitalized for a long period. Eventually, when able to gain mobility he discovered that facing a large congregation was causing problems. Since the church was smaller at Rhyl and the demands less, he decided it was time for a change. But after ministering there for a year, he received an invitation to join Granada Television — they were starting a Welsh service. He accepted, and went to work with the company in Manchester. There, as he was a script-writer and producer, the process of writing which up to then had been a hobby, became professional work. Another inducement of a totally different kind was the inspiring influence of some north Wales poets: Gwilym R. Jones, Mathonwy Hughes and Huw T. Edwards. As with the Cadwgan circle, Rhydwen co-published several poems with these in a volume of verse bearing the title AR Y CYD *(Together)*.

In 1964 Rhydwen won the National Crown for the second time. The Eisteddfod was at Swansea and the subject 'Ffynhonnau' *(Springs)*. The decision of the adjudicators this time was far from being the unanimous verdict it had been in Mountain Ash. In fact it was an exceedingly mixed one. Out of thirty-one competitors, Sir T. H. Parry-Williams wished to crown John Roderick Rees for his *pryddest* on the rural life

24

around Mynydd Bach and Bethania in Cardiganshire. Eirian Davies, on the other hand, decisively favoured Rhydwen's poem which portrayed the changing life and society of the Rhondda in the twentieth century. The third adjudicator, W. J. Gruffydd, wanted to award the Crown to Rhydwen, but suggested sharing the £60 money prize between him and John Roderick Rees. (A decision of this nature in the Crown competition was not unprecedented in the Eisteddfod's history, since it had occurred once before in the Rhyl Festival of 1892, when the two adjudicators, Elis Wyn of Gwyrfai and Cadfan, gave the Crown to Iolo Caernarfon, but shared the £20 cash reward between him and Ben Davies, Panteg.) However in Swansea the Eisteddfod officials decided that the Crown and the whole sum of money be given to the poet adjudged best by two of the three adjudicators, a narrow victory.

Despite the lack of unanimity amongst the adjudicators, Rhydwen's *pryddest*, described by Sir T. H. Parry-Williams as a dramatic composition for voices, is generally regarded as one of the best Crown poems ever. He dedicated it to the children of Ynys-Wen Welsh School in memory of three of their worthies — John Robert Williams, a collier and a poet; Robert Griffiths, pastor and minister; James Kitchener Davies, teacher, author and politician. As Eirian Davies remarked: *These were the springs of the Welsh life that watered the parched land in barren times, and the lives of the three now a living stream through the children of the Welsh School of Ynys-Wen.*

At the outset, the recollections of a few old natives about the three remind the poet, the work's main narrating voice, of childhood and pre-industrial days when nature held sway and the people led a tough, slow, patient life in close communion with the earth:

> 'Roedd eu bara'n fynych yn wlân ar ddraenen bigog,
> A'u gweddi'n fodrwy o fysedd am dethau'r fuwch . . .
> Yma, ar dir eu gwlad, a'u dillad yn dyllog,
> A'r cnawd wedi'i lapio'n dynn am yr esgyrn diwyd,
> Bref a chân a pharabl dyfroedd yn unig ar eu clyw,
> Disgwyliai'r werin amyneddgar
> I groesawu'r llo ar ddyfod yn feddw o'r groth,
> A sychu'r oen newydd-sbon yn diferu o fywyd,
> A golchi'r clwy' ar ais y gaseg neu bwrs y fuwch;
> Yma, lle 'roedd y ffynhonnau mor bur â'r bobl,
> A'r ffrydiau mor siriol â'r plant
> Yn canu eu diniweidrwydd drwy'r Cwm.

(Their daily bread fleece on a barbed fence,
and their prayer a bunch of fingers under the cow's udder . . .
Here, on native soil, their garments threadbare,
and the flesh taut around the hard-working bone,
only the lowing of cattle, bird song and the murmur of waters to
        be heard,
a patient people waited
to greet the calf come tipsy out of the womb
and wipe the new-born lamb dripping with life,
and wash the wound on the side of the mare or the purse of the
        cow;
here, where the streams were as pure as the people,
and their flow as merry as the children
who sang their innocence over these hills.)

(Translated by Rhydwen Williams — RHONDDA POEMS)

At the beginning of the third section the narrator illustrates in question form the havoc which industry had wrought on forests, bird life and the purity of the river. But, alternatively, colloquial voices dwell on the heyday of the valley, and the cultural and rebellious life around the coal-pits. Nevertheless, in reality, Welshness and social coherence had crumbled underneath the Anglicization and uprooting of the new era: jazz bands came to Blaenclydach, and the girl whose mother sang in Evan Roberts's Revival danced like Carmen with a *red rose in her mouth*:

Nid addurn yw ein Cymreictod ond brwydr.
Nid difyrrwch, ond iau ar ein gwarrau.
(Mae'r iau yn drom. Mae'r frwydr heb fwrw-arfau).
Daeth y gegin-gawl i wawdio'n tlodi.
Prynwyd urddas oddi arnom â cheiniogau'r dôl.
Diwreiddiwyd ni wrth y cannoedd. Ail-blannwyd ar draws
    y byd —
Hen wreiddiau diwerth a dyf ar unrhyw domen dan haul.

— Ma' Morgan wedi cael B.A.
— Neis 'u gweld nhw'n dod mlan.
— Ma' Megan wedi cael headship yn Stoke.
— Roedd hi'n dda gyta'r plant yn Saron.
— Ma' Percy yn giwrat yn Stepney.
— Siwtio'r elite i'r dim.
— Ma' Dyfrig yn male nurse yn Uttoxeter.
— Bydd Tommy Farr gystal bachan â Tom Thomas.
— Os caiff Jimmy Myrphy'i le gyta West Brom.
Pwy fydd ar ôl ar y mynyddoedd hyn
I rydu gyda'r gêr a'r olwynion a'r rheiliau,
A heneiddio gyda'r Achos a'r Cymmrodorion a'r Iaith
Fel hen ieir yn crafu eu bywoliaeth yn rwbel y blynyddoedd?

(Our nationhood is not an adornment but a struggle;
not entertainment, but a yoke we carry.
the yoke is heavy and there is no relief!
We saw the soup-kitchen aggravate our poverty.
our dignity bought with the pittance of the dole;
uprooted by the hundreds, we were transplanted all over the
    world —
feeble old roots that would grow on any dump under the sun!

— Our Morgan 'ave 'ad 'is B.A.
— Oh, there's nice to see them gettin' on in the world!
— Our Megan 'ave 'ad a headship in Stoke!
— Well, she was always good with the children in Saron.
— Our Percy is now a curate in Stepney!
— Oh, he'll suit the elite to the T!
— Our Dyfrig is a male-nurse in Uttoxeter!
— I think Tommy Farr will be as good as Tom Thomas.
— And if Jimmy Murphy gets a chance with West Brom. —
Who will be left on these hills
to rust with the gear and the rails and the wheels
and grow old with the Chapel and the Cymmrodorion and the
*   mother-tongue,*
scratching a living like old hens in the rubble of past years?)

(Translated by Rhydwen Williams — RHONDDA POEMS)

But, according to the final section, this struggle typified by the unyielding spirit of the three seems to be bearing fruit, while all the tumult and activity of the industrial days have disappeared. Here, the rebirth of hope and the resurgence of a new life for the valley is joyfully announced: there are new lovers in the heather of Moel Cadwgan, the birds and fish return avidly to the trees and the streams, and fresh apples swelling in Pentwyn's orchard. The mirth of waters is audible again and the *pryddest* ends on a positive confident note:

> *— Gŵr dierth?*
> *— Ie.*
> *Eisteddai ar sedd wrth odre Moel Cadwgan.*
> *Cap. Ffon. Sigaret.*
> *Rhyw led-gofio'i wyneb. Hynny oedd ar ôl ohono.*
> *— Ma' plant y ferch 'cw yn mynd i'r Ysgol Gymraeg.*
> *— Ma' 'na fachan ifanc o'r coleg yn dod i Nebo.*
> *Trodd dros y trum—yn her i bryder bro.*
> *A'i ffon mor gadarn â'i ffydd.*

(— *Stranger?*
— *Yes.*
He was seated at the foot of Moel Cadwgan.
Cap. Stick. Cigarette.
I seemed to remember his face — what was left.
— *My daughter's girl goes to the Welsh School now.*
— *A young man come to our chapel straight from the college.*
He made to go — as though defying a valley's fears.
His stick as firm as his faith.)

(Translated by Rhydwen Williams — RHONDDA POEMS)

'Ffynhonnau' is a significant poem. The impressive echoes of the pulpit are clearly audible in the rhythms of the main voice, and the dramatic character of several sections reflects Rhydwen's experience in the world of radio and television. Sir T. H. Parry-Williams noted that the imperative form *Gwrandewch* which occurs often at the beginning of stanzas is reminiscent of the use which Dylan Thomas made of *Hush* and *Listen* in UNDER MILK WOOD, but the poet himself insists that its source, in his case, was in the New Testament: *Gwrandewch: Wele, heuwr a aeth allan i hau (Listen! A sower went out to sow).* But most importantly it heralds the spiritual return of the poet to his beloved Rhondda. Soon he was to return, settling in Aberdare to fulfil himself as a full-time writer and record the past of his native valley. 'Ffynhonnau' was the first of the new output; it was with this epic-poem he began his literary vocation in earnest.

IV

In 1965, Barddoniaeth Rhydwen Williams appeared. One of the main attractions of the volume is the easy-mannered conversational style of its narrative portrayals. Basically, these poems, in accordance with one of the main themes of Welsh poetry since the sixth century, are eulogies, songs of praise to the humanity and resistance of mining folk during the depression years. For example, Uncle Siôn had a source of inner strength to withstand the dreariness and deprivations which turned life for most men into a long drawn-out monotony:

'Roedd gan bawb ar y mynydd ei ddiddordeb—cadw moch neu
        gadw milgwn,
Chwythu trombôn, taflu coeten, magu adar-sioe;
A phan ddaeth dyddiau'r dirwasgiad a phob awr yn faith gan
        segurdod,
Amlygodd ambell un athrylith am guro pêl yn erbyn talcen tŷ.
Ond aeth f'ewyrth drwy holl gyfnodau ffyrnig Cwm Rhondda—
Berw ysbrydol Evan Roberts a gwasgfa faterol y Streic Fawr,
Militariaeth 1914 a phrês-rwydd ffatrïoedd 1941—
Heb i ddim ei ddenu oddi wrth amyneddgar grefft ei awen,
Hen gwmnïaeth awdur, a chyfaredd gwyrthiau'r Gymraeg.

(People on the mountain had their interests—
keeping pigs or whippets,
blowing a trombone, playing quoits, rearing pigeons,
and when the Depression came, hours unbearable and boring,
some would display a genius for hand-ball or the gazooka!
But my uncle went through all the ravages of the valley —
Evan Roberts' Revival and the '26 Strike,
the dark days of 1914 and the dark days of 1941,

nothing distracting him from the patient craft of his poem,
a good book, and the miracle of his mother-tongue.)

(Translated by Rhydwen Williams — RHONDDA POEMS)

In 'Y Ddau' (*The Two*) the poet rejoices that his parents managed to keep their deep-rooted honour through the agonizing years. Again, in 'Dychwelyd' *(Return)* two elderly sisters pay their last visit to the old home in Nazareth, Gwynedd with quiet dignity despite a long life of sorrow and trials. 'John Mathews' relates the story of an old gentle negro who came to the Rhondda during the poet's boyhood:

...Edrychwn ar yr wyneb eboni,
y llygaid gwylaidd,
y gwythiennau'n gweithio'n ei wddw wrth ganu,
yr ên gyntefig yn crynu â'r llawenydd sydd ar gael ymysg
*   angylion Duw,*
a'r gwefusau du'n symud fel malwod mawr —
'roeddwn fel un yn gweld y wawr yn torri trwy'r gilfach,
cilfach o wayw hynafol, dinistriol du;
'roeddwn fel un yn edrych ar yr wyneb cynta' a wenodd
*   erioed,*
dieithr fel rhith, cynefin fel darn o lo,
a'r diniweidrwydd a gollwyd yn Eden,
a'r perffeithrwydd a laddwyd ar y Pren,
a'r daioni amyneddgar a ffrwydrodd yr Ogof ar agor gynt,
oll ar gael yn yr wyneb ysol, oesoesol hwn.

(And I would stare at the ebony face,
the humility of the eyes,
the veins of the neck throbbing with song,
and the primitive jaw trembling with the joy amongst God's
*   angels,*
and black lips moving like large snails.
It was as though I was seeing the dawn break in a ravine,

31

a ravine darkened with inhumanity;
it was as though I was seeing the first smile
that ever lit the face of man,
stranger than an apparition,
more familiar than the face of coal,
and the innocence lost in Eden,
and the loveliness slain on a Tree,
and the patient virtues that burst open the Tomb,
all peering in this one unassuming, consuming face.)

(Translated by Rhydwen Williams — RHONDDA POEMS)

One other poem of considerable merit which may be included in this category is 'Nadolig' *(Christmas)* which Rhydwen wrote for his son, Huw. Here the sanctity and natural ecstasy of a child's Christmas is examined, a rapture and a purity which the poet finds impossible to re-enter and recapture from the unimaginative and disillusioned world of manhood:

Minnau, ni welaf Gwlifer yn gaeth na Sinderela'n ei rhacs;
cerddaf luwch-eira'r Nadoligau. Ail-geisiaf yr ias.
Ond cracia di'r craceri, Huw bach! . . . Mae'n Nadolig eto.

(Myself, I cannot see Gulliver in fetters nor Cinderella in rags;
I walk the snow-drift of Christmases. I seek again the thrill.
Pull the crackers, little fellow! . . . It's Christmas again.)

The volume contains a few poems to some well-known poets of Wales. In 'Robert Williams Parry' the poet's moment of death is depicted by striking metaphors: the silence fills the senses, the muse bidding farewell to the mind, and his body emptied under the imperialism of death. This poem exploits the imagery of Auden's famous lament 'In Memory of W. B. Yeats'. Another poem, a loosely constructed sonnet, pictures Dylan Thomas as a wondrous laden

32

galleon venturing on a new course across a timeless sea. The best poem in this category, and indeed one of the most effective of all Rhydwen's verse, is the one titled 'Kitch', James Kitchener Davies. A great scope of admiration and grief is disciplined here by tense, tight diction:

> Cariad mwy creulon
> Na phoen a phangau,
> Sy'n dechrau'n angerdd
> A diweddu'n angau . . .
>
> Caru llên a thraddod,
> Meddwl a moes
> A gwneuthur ohonynt
> Ein credo a'n croes . . .
>
> A chrefu hefyd,
> Er mwyn ein dydd,
> Y clasuron o'r clai
> A'r breuddwydion o'r pridd.
>
> (Love more cruel
> Than pain and pangs;
> Begins as passion
> And ends in death . . .
>
> Loving tradition,
> Intellect and ethics
> And from them creating
> Our creed and cross . . .
>
> An imploring too
> On behalf of our times,
> The classics from the clay
> And the dreams from the soil.)

Another basic theme is the deep-seated attachment

shown towards animals. These are vivacious loving poems and at times jocularly critical. For Rhydwen, animals have special faculties — an original inner and outer beauty and an admirable robustness: 'Y Llewpart' *(The Leopard)* is praised for his *silent ferocity, symmetrical stability and concise primitiveness*:

> *Goroesodd hwn y gwareiddidau heb golli min ei ewinedd*
> *nac ildio'i arglwyddiaeth anifeilaidd*
> *i ymddiried mewn dyn . . .*

> *(He has survived civilizations without losing the sharpness of*
>   *talons*
> *nor yielding his beastly dominion*
> *to trust man . . .)*

'Yr Eliffant' is a delightful poem which attributes nobility and patience to the ancient pachyderm as he carries a load of children for a joy-ride. It is significant that 'Y Babwn', the creature nearest to man in appearance and nature is viewed compassionately, yet in terms akin to ridicule. He is depicted lonely, abandoned like an astronaut, fingering his own organs, the complete opposite of the classical tiger and the magnificent elephant. The baboon's behaviour is a symbol of man's meaningless existence on earth, despite his progress and many achievements:

> *Daeth arogl heibio'i drwyn,*
> *arogl o'r gwair a'r cagl,*
> *a'i ddeffro i'w ffolennau ei hun,*
> *a'i yrru fel rhoced a'i din ar dân*
> *yn orbid sbeitlyd Rhyw.*
> *A phan welais ei wyneb wedyn — O dristwch*
>   *chwerthinllyd —*
> *gwelais yr holl aparatws nerfus*
> *a siwrneiodd erioed hen fapiau celf a chân*

34

yn un cnotyn anobeithiol,
yn byw i ddiawl o ddim
ar wahân i'r orchest derfynol fawr
o bigo trwyn.

(A smell wafted to his nose,
a smell from the hay and dung
to make him conscious of his loins,
and drive him like a rocket, his rump on fire,
on the spiteful orbit of Sex.
And when I saw his face again — O laughable sadness —
I perceived the entire nervous apparatus
which has always travelled the old paths of art and song
as a hopeless knot,
living for sod all
except the great final accomplishment
of picking his nose.)

'Y March' *(The Stallion)* glorifies the strength and sheer force of animality. The horse is seen as a creature out of antiquity, an extension of the natural world, a wiry animal resembling a moving chunk of rock or a wandering meteor. Alan Llwyd has commented on the undeniable similarity of the poem to Edwin Muir's 'Horses': *a machinelike body in a brilliant charge of carnality, his shoes' thud hammering the grass like nails into the clay.* Indeed, similarity to another poem, 'The Horses', by the same poet may be discerned here, but the intensity of expression, and the nature of the empathic scope is most certainly original:

Heddiw, yr oedd holl brydferthwch ei ganrifoedd, o'i fwng i'w
        bigwrn,
ei gynaeafau a'i ryfeloedd a'i ffeiriau a'i gaethiwed yn y
        talcen-glo,
y cwbl yn chwys-domen-dail o gnawdol,
ac yn apocaluptaidd fyw.

(Today, his centuries of beauty, from mane to fetlock,
his harvests and wars and fairs and captivity in the coal-pit,
all a steaming pile of flesh,
and apocalyptically alive.)

Another exceedingly striking poem where an animal is of central importance is the sonnet 'Moduro' *(Motoring)*, but here the creature, a rabbit, is at the deadly receiving-end of man's modern tempo of life. The *furry bundle* suddenly appears in the headlights of the poet's speeding car on the road *from Flint to Frith*. The instantaneous skidding build-up to the collision is conveyed in language of screeching tension:

> *Trigain milltir yr awr! Rhy hwyr bryd hyn!*
> *Car a chwningen a'u silindrau i gyd yn crynu.*

> *(Sixty miles an hour! Too late at such speed!*
> *Car and rabbit vibrating, all cylinders revving.)*

The expression of the death-blow is a powerful ago-nizing protest against man's impulsive, reckless nature:

> *Yn nes . . . yn nes . . . yn nes — a'r corffilyn yn llenwi'r llawr*
> *A'r ddau lygad bach wrth ddiffodd yn boddi'r lampau mawr.*

(Nearer...nearer...nearer — and the puny body overwhelms the
highway
And the two small eyes as their light went out dimming the mighty
headlamps.)

Y FFYNHONNAU A CHERDDI ERAILL appeared in 1970. The freshest aspect of this volume is the poet's concern for the future of the nation and its language. His outlook is scathing and of a pessimistic nature. He is critical of the unperturbed attitude of the older generation at a time when the youth of Wales were leading a spirited campaign for equal status for their language in response to the historic radio lecture 'Tynged yr Iaith' *(The Fate of the Language)* by Saunders Lewis in February 1962:

Pan oedd y dydd yn las a'r cymylau mor ysgafn â hancesi,
plethai'r adar eu hadenydd a phlygu'r gwyntoedd â'u plu;
gorweddai'r bryniau, rhes ar ôl rhes, fel crasiad cynnes o dorthau,
a ninnau'n ein byd bach dof . . . heb wybod fod terfysg yn y tir.

Hen fel rhai, pan yw'r utgorn yn galw, sy'n rhy fyddar i falio;
hen fel rhai, pan yw'r meirch wrth y pyrth, sy'n rhy ddall i
    weld y llwch;
hen fel rhai, pan yw'r treiswyr yn taro, sy'n rhy fud i erfyn a
    gweddïo;
hen hen hen . . . pan yw'r genedl yn dod i'w hoed.

(When the day was blue and clouds as flimsy as handkerchiefs,
birds plaited wings and bent the wind with their feathers;
the hills relaxed, row after row, like a line of newly baked loaves,
and we in our snug little world . . . oblivious to the tumult in the
    land.

Old like those, when the trumpet calls, too deaf to hear;
old like those, steeds at the gate, too blind to see the dust;
old like those, at the time of rape, too mute to plead and pray;
old old old . . . when a nation comes of age.)

In 'Cymru' the entire land, all its beauty, history and tradition appears unreal, a country of ghostlike objects and shadowy voices. *Cymru* is without pride, dreams or faith; all she can do now is exist prudently and submit to her overlords. The hills and temples are gone into the hands of strangers; only the dead, from their graves, can now announce her former glory. The picture is a dark one. In 'Capelau' the language is an alien among the hills, and the old strongholds are in ruins and up for sale.

However, Rhydwen explicitly believes that the arts and old values have an enlivening role to play, and regards the artist more fundamental than anyone in the battle for survival. In the poem to Huw, 'H.R.W.', on his twenty-first birthday, the poet implores:

Fy mab, gwna dy gariadferch
Yn rhan o'r bryniau diymhongar hyn,
Rhag ofn nad oes ond odlau bardd a lliwiau pob ryw beintiwr bach
A geidw'r gogoniant — Cymru!
Ar ôl i Dryweryn a Chlywedog
A'r ardaloedd i gyd fynd dan y dŵr!

(My son, make your art
A part of these humble hills.
Lest there is only a poet's rhymes and colours of little painters
To salvage the glory — Wales!
After Tryweryn and Clywedog
And all our communities have gone under water!)

The same urgency is implied in the poem to Dr Kate Roberts, one of the guardians of our inheritance. Her home has been solidly put together like one of her stories. She is an active supporter of our institutions — the Welsh School, the Cymmrodorion and a Sunday-school teacher. Above all she is an artist with the imagination and sensitivity to transform her manuscript into a treasure comparable with the Red Book of Hergest or the Black Book of Carmarthen. She is the perpetuator of the culture of her race, a prolonger of its life.

In his third book of verse, Y CHWYLDRO GWYRDD, *(The Green Revolution)*, published in 1972, Rhydwen penetrates through the encircling negativity and gloom of the struggle to exist to the presence of the uninterrupted flow of Life itself. The series of prayers which has given its title to the volume begs the Word to reinvigorate life on Cadwgan mountain: to restore the beauty of its streams, renew the sap of the ailing trees, *and release songbirds in a shower of music* over the valley. Above all the poet pleads a renaissance on the drab land and its people, the central theme of his vision:

> *a llefara, llefara, uwch y gelain sorth, Seisnigaidd hon*
> *a'i galw i ryddhad yr atgyfodiad gwyrdd!*

> *(and speak, speak, above this drowsy, Saxon corpse*
> *and call her to the emancipation of this green resurrection!)*

In 'Tachwedd', a cruel severe month, the people huddle together in a cold rainy climate, till eventually the feebleness of man is bathed in the glory of the truth, depicted in the tearing light of a thunderstorm. The impregnable power of life dawns on the poet where the stump of an old tree on Cadwgan, which has survived the upheavals of generations, is seen as an indestructable remnant of the valley's life still clinging to its scorched patch of earth:

> *Na, ni thyf hon flodau ac nid estyn afalau i neb, dim ond*
> *dangos ei chorff a'i bronnau noeth i bawb ar ochr y ffordd fel*
> *hyn mor glasurol ag un o gerfluniau'r Lourve, rhyw dorso o*
> *berffeithrwydd wedi goroesi pob newid a chwalfa, yn gwneud*
> *   dim*
> *mwy na rhoi cysgod i ddafad a chrwydryn ar dro ac yn glynu*
> *am ei bywyd wrth yr hen Gwm 'ma â'i gwreiddiau gwancus.*

(No, this tree grows no flowers nor offers fruit in season,
displaying only body and breasts by the roadside as
classical as any of the Louvre's statues, a perfect torso
having survived change and catastrophe, and doing nothing
other than giving shelter to a sheep and a tramp, holding
on for all her might to this old hill with lustful roots.)

'Ecce Homo' is a natural climax to the ascent of such
a vision. Here the sustainer of life is named and His
message interpreted as the inspiration of all small
peoples on earth:

Wrth ei bobl, dywedodd: 'Os y Mab gan hynny a'ch rhyddha . . .'
ac ar y gair, cysegrwyd Mudiad Rhyddid pob cenedl fach dan
*   haul.*
Galwodd un o'r selotiaid yn ddisgybl, ac yn yr act,
aeth cenedlaetholdeb yn rhan o bolisi Teyrnas Dduw.
Chwipiodd yr offeiriaid a'r dynion-busnes; ac o'r pryd hwnnw
*   ymlaen,*
aeth cyfaddawd â'r pwerau mawr yn ffieidd-dra ar allor Duw.

(To his followers, he said: 'If the Son shall make you free . . .'
instantly, the Freedom Movement of every small kingdom under
*   the sun was sanctified.*
He summoned a zealot as a disciple, and by doing so,
nationhood became the policy of God's Kingdom.
He slashed the priests and merchants; and from that time hence,
compromise with the great powers became an abomination on
*   God's altar.)*

Christ's sense of nationhood has been underesti-
mated. It was this rebellious stance, with its political
implication often, rather than His new religious
emphasis that posed a threat to the authorities.
Ultimately, it was the cause of His death, and such
treachery still threatens:

Mae'r Gwirionedd ar ein pyst ninnau heddiw,
a'r Gwaed ar ein harwyddion yfflon a'r pelmynt poen.

(The Truth is on our lintels today,
and Blood on our torn road signs and anguished pavements.)

Wales and Israel are still under duress. Rhydwen sees a similarity between the faith of such a visionary as Lewis Valentine and the Hebrew psalmist; sorrow was in the soul of both. The last couplet of the eulogy to Valentine crystallizes the interpretation:

Gorchfygodd ei elynion trwy fod yn ostyngedig,
a rhoddodd daw ar ei feirniaid trwy fod yn fud.

(He overcame his enemies by his humility,
and silenced his critics by being mute.)

V

From 1972 to 1979 Rhydwen Williams produced five
books, four prose works and one volume of poetry.
The first, BREUDDWYD RHONABWY JONES (*The Dream of
Rhonabwy Jones*), is a short novel, roughly based on
Orwell's ANIMAL FARM where creatures rule the earth
as an alternative to man. But there is, none the less, a
major difference between the two. Orwell's story is a
biting satire of curt terse prose on dictatorship. The
animals' revolution, like the tyrannical human rule
before it, had within it, from the beginning, the same
old seeds of oppression and self-destruction, and its
manifestations of them are traced, step by step, until
its final degeneration into a fully-fledged totalitarian-
ism. In Rhydwen's novel, a light-hearted work of teas-
ing good humour, the animals are successful in their
attempt to govern Wales after the failures of
Westminster and its consequent disbanding.
Rhonabwy Jones sees an exciting experiment in
progress through *the crack in the universe*: the banish-
ment of all money, the cause of man's downfall; the
depollution of Wales; the formation of New Welsh; the
beginning of a unique National Eisteddfod producing
original literature; precedence given to the act of worship over preaching. Even the jackdaw's greedy
attempt to recover the buried money was not sufficent
to overthrow the new aspiring system. All in all,
BREUDDWYD RHONABWY JONES possesses the mood of a
deeply cherished vision.

The contrast can be accounted for in the light of several factors. The novel's blurb reveals one of them: *At*

the end of the first chapter of Genesis the following remark is seen, 'and behold, it was very good'; God in his element having created the world. By the sixth chapter, he is not so happy — 'And the Lord was sorry that he had made man on earth'. A verse later, he decides to drown the entire species except for one family which was allowed to go a-sailing. It is true that he repented afterwards but it is more than possible that even God can change his mind. What if he decides to give it another try, abolish humans from the planet and putting the animals to govern? The comment explains why the animals, different from Orwell's creatures, do not have to fight to remove man from their territory; the stage is vacant for them, much to their surprise, to start their revolutionary administration. Again, although the vision of a man-free land is revealed in a dream to Major the Pig in ANIMAL FARM, the title of Rhydwen's story comes from the thirteenth-century Welsh tale, 'Breuddwyd Rhonabwy'. It is also interesting to note that one of the functions of the dream which Rhonabwy had was to disclose the vast difference between the grandeur of Arthur's age and the fading glory of medieval Powys, denoting the contrast between two different ruling powers. This plot must have reminded Rhydwen of other relative references, things like the part played by wild life in the release of Mabon son of Modron in 'Culhwch ac Olwen', and R. Williams Parry's well-known sonnet 'Rhyfeddodau'r Wawr' (*Wonders of the Dawn*) where the delights of an early morning summer scene are lovingly described, and the desire for the removal of man and his industrial pollution expressed. Rhydwen himself had also touched on this theme in his delightful poem 'Yn Nheyrnas Diniweidrwydd' (*In the Kingdom of Innocence*) where is envisaged the kind of paradise which he yearns to see appearing on earth:

Yn nheyrnas diniweidrwydd,
Mae pawb o'r un un ach;
Pob bychan fel pe'n frenin,
Pob brenin fel un bach.
Mae'r ych a'r ebol-asyn,
Y syml a'r doeth yn un;
A'r thus a'r myrr a'r hatling
Heb arwydd p'un yw p'un.

(In the kingdom of innocence,
All are of one and the same stock;
Every babe as a king,
Every king as a babe.
The ox and the donkey,
The wise and simple one;
And the frankincense, the myrrh and the mite
With nothing to tell them apart.)

Also, if one connects Rhydwen's strong personal fond-
ness for all forms of animal life with the above literary considerations it is no wonder that his story is so
different from that of ANIMAL FARM.

YSTLUMOD *(Bats)*, a series of nineteen *vers libre* poems
commissioned for television, is reminiscent of Ted
Hughes's *Crow*, but their basic feature is quite different. *Crow* depicts life as a voracious existence being
wholly guided by primordial instincts in a ruthless
and godless world; YSTLUMOD is a satire on human fol-
lies, deceitfulness and loathsome morality.
Rhydwen's bat, a creation of pathos and comedy, ironically evolves to emulate man. The Creator whom he
visualizes is nothing more than a reflection of his own
form and temperament. He develops language for the
purpose of becoming a *civilized vampire*. He also realizes that concentrating on activities like writing poetry
is completely useless, whilst specializing in useful

44

chores such as painting a door or mixing cement is a
sure way of being paid handsomely:

> Fin hwyr, ar ôl swpera, cyn mentro i'r nos,
> arferai Ystlum fynd am dro o'r neilltu . . .
> (Mae amser pan yw'n dda i ddyn ac ystlum fod ar ei ben ei
>   hun!)
> a sylweddolodd fod ei bererindodau erbyn hyn
> wedi codi tomen yn yr ardal gymaint â thip-glo.
> 'Guano! Guano!', gweiddodd, pan welodd y twr uchel
>   echretaidd.
> Oedd! Roedd yntau yn medru cynhyrchu.
> Onid oedd holl erddi a gwinllanoedd y ddaear yn aros i'w
>   gwrteithio?
> Y mae 'mynd' ar ei ddiwydiant hyd y dwthwn hwn.

(At dusk, after supper, before risking abroad,
Bat used to retire for a stroll . . .
(There's a time when it's good for bat and man to be alone!)
and he realized that his visitations by now
had raised a heap in the district as high as a coal tip.
'Guano! Guano!', he cried, when he saw the high tower of
      excreta.
Yes! He too could produce.
Were not all the orchards and vineyards on earth waiting to be
      manured?
There's a demand for such industry till today.)

It also dawns on him, under interesting circumstances,
that man's religion is only a layer of godliness cover-
ing a primitive basic nature. The bat, apparently, went
to Zion often on the Sabbath for an undisturbed rest,
but he was spotted, on one occasion, by the worship-
pers who instantly raved for the blood of the ugly devil
within their hallowed precincts. He escaped with the
conclusion that instinct is more trustworthy than
grace.

Finally, the bat learns about the sick priorities of mankind. Although he had literary abilities he would be remembered in history for another much more valuable contribution — killing billions of midges:

Mae gŵr a fynn lunio'i gerdd,
amddiffyn iaith, arddel y gwir,
o flaen lladd gwybed mewn trwbwl.
Hwyr neu hwyrach, bydd gan yr awdurdodau warant i'w
*   restio,*
plismyn gewynnog yn barod i gydio ynddo,
a meddyg wrth law i dystio nad yw'n gall.

Rhoes Saunders a Solzhenitsyn eu clasuron i'w cenhedloedd,
ond deil dynion i daeru eu bod yn hongian wrth ewin yn y niwl
ac yn edrych yn dindrosben ar y byd!

  (The man who wants to write a poem,
  defend a language, acknowledge the truth,
  instead of killing midges is in trouble.
  Sooner or later, the authorities will have a warrant to arrest.
  muscular policemen ready to grab,
  and a doctor to certify him.

  Saunders and Solzhenitsyn gave classics to their nations,
  but men still insist they were hanging by a nail in the fog
  and looking upside-down on the world!)

Man is a belligerent being; the big powers are a ridiculous circle; Belfast and Vietnam are under military oppression; a prime minister flies with the good wish of a Queen; the president announces God and Billy Graham are well pleased; a judge loves Wales but opposes destroying English road signs. The bat strongly realizes, in such alien surroundings, that his own species with its separate territory and identity is an inheritance to be resolutely defended:

46

Mae'n wir nad oes gennym ni ddim ar ein helw,
meddyliodd, dim ond —
ogofau
cilfachau
toeau
trawstiau
gweoedd
beddau
gwyll;
eto i gyd, mae —
pob trawst i'w amddiffyn
pob gwe i'w gwarchod
pob ogof i'w chadw
pob cilfach yn etifeddiaeth!

(It is true that we possess nothing,
he thought, nothing except —
caves
nooks
roofs
beams
webs
graves
gloom;
nevertheless
every rafter must be protected
every web guarded
every cave preserved
every cranny an inheritance!)

YSTLUMOD, different from *Crow's* complete break with normal impressions and landscapes, is a human composition; it focuses on human emotions and positive aspirations. Although man is constantly guilty of extreme foolishness, he is not without his true and noble values, the wealth of his higher faculties — genuine Christianity and nationalism, for instance, qualities to be devotedly cherished, but yet priority always seems to be blatantly given to idiotic intentions and ridiculous considerations. That is the essential caustic message of YSTLUMOD,

THE ANGRY VINEYARD, Rhydwen's English language novel is his most powerful prose work. (Its first draft was in Welsh bearing the title CAMWEDD, and by now that version has been completed by Huw Ithel). It deals with the Merthyr riots of 1831, as does THE FIRE PEOPLE by Alexander Cordell. In THE ANGRY VINEYARD, a high degree of exciting and sensitive narration is achieved by empathically highlighting the plight of the Merthyr proletariat under the despotism of William Crawshay, the iron master of Cyfarthfa. Wholehearted imaginative sympathy is shown with the close-knitted common people in scene after scene of strife, extreme distress and heart-rending deaths. All of this probably stems from the fact that this time the author had found a stirring tragic episode of industrial life outside the confines and influence of his own family circle and contemporaries, and yet just the right connective distance in time from the grieving colliers and ironworkers of 1831 to be able to identify himself fully with their cause more as a pure novelist than a social story-teller. It is an ironic coincidence that his parents had to leave the Rhondda valley exactly a century to the year of the Merthyr insurrection. In other words, they were forced to celebrate the centenary of their past fellow-workers with precisely the same brand of economic suffering.

THE ANGRY VINEYARD, has been written from an uncompromising Welsh viewpoint. Its very title suggests a zealous fellow-feeling with Saunders Lewis's vision of Wales as a violated vineyard in BUCHEDD GARMON. This aspect is the one big difference between

it and THE FIRE PEOPLE which, although equally moving, is more objective and international in character.
Rhydwen interprets the agitation at Merthyr as an
upsurge of a new political consciousness in a down-
trodden people. In the prologue he states that *the struggle was for more than wages and better hours and even the
reform of the structure of Parliament, but for their survival
as a nation.* And what was more, the tyrant of Cyfarthfa
was only too aware of the significance of the new
thrilling turmoil which the Welsh pamphleteers of the
day were constantly provoking amongst the workers.
Dic Penderyn, the people's champion and the main
instigator for reform, realized that as far as the Welsh
were concerned neither the Whigs nor the Tories were
likely to offer any form of relief. Therefore the common people had to unite forces against the government. The movement had the unmistakable
undertones of a national revolt. Lewsyn yr Heliwr,
another of its prominent figures, viewed the English
law askance; the merciless plundering of the bailiffs
amongst working-class homes instinctively infuriated
his naturally inflammatory Welsh blood. Even members of the Highland Regiment on their march to quell
the uprising felt a deep-seated sympathy with the
Merthyr trouble-makers: their own forefathers, as
well, had had to fight perpetually against the same
English pillager. The basic fervour behind the rebellion is passionately summed up by Dic Penderyn in
his cell at Cardiff prison:

*The Welsh people are without dignity in their own land. Their
hills are scorched and their bodies taxed to yield a wealth in which
they have no share. Their language is the prattle of beggars fit
only to form apologies to the mighty and supplications to the
Almighty, and one to be hushed immediately their betters begin
to talk in English. When the legs of the old women and the skull*

of the small boy cracked under the hooves outside the Castle Inn,
it was a nation that those horses trampled then. And so the ques-
tion is, not whether a death on the gallows will sober the people,
but whether it will take more than a few smashed windows to
bring the masters to their senses. If one life is to be forfeited to
make Crawshay, Guest, Hill, and the others, feel safer and
stronger, then it is a scandal; but if my death could ever rouse my
people out of their helplessness enough to see themselves as a peo-
ple, equal under the sun with all the peoples of the world, and not
the mute patient, half-starved drudges of a master who maintains
his omnipotence through the utter weakness of others, then . . .
all is well. If my death only destroys me, then it is a shame; but
if it is the beginning of the destruction of the order that keeps my
people in chains, the terrible chains of suffering and poverty and
humiliation and scorn, then it is worthwhile.

APOLO and GALLT Y GOFAL (*Hill of Tribulation*) are two
psychological novelettes, in the sense that the chief
character of each one shows personality perversive-
ness and emotional disturbances which end in suicide.
Dr John Rowlands mentioned in a radio lecture on the
Welsh novel that more novels written around the contemporary scene would be welcomed. APOLO is such
a creation, Rhydwen's first step in prose from the
realm of industrial history to present day life. Its set-
ting is a television headquarters and studio, surroundings with which the author was very familiar.
The picture drawn is an extremely vitriolic one. One
reviewer with an extensive experience of the television world, Euryn Ogwen Williams, stated that he had
never met anyone in the television industry who
entirely resembled a single character portrayed in
APOLO According to him the characters exceed the
frontiers of flesh and blood, and APOLO was not a
novel, in the usual sense of the word, but a part of the
mythology of the twentieth century, the Mabinogi of
television circles. But, be that as it may, the underly-

ing purpose of the author is only too obvious: to reveal the insensitive, impersonal, scheming and power-hungry nature of life within a large television company. In fact, the portrayal of John Merlin, the chairman and dictator of Apolo, is an image of a man indulging in a highly artificial, narcissistic and mega-lomaniac type of behaviour. As one of his acquaintances remarked about his fatal delusions of grandeur: *'John wanted to be lord, poor fellow! And he wasn't big enough, I'm afraid!'* The novelette mocks and rejects such madness. John Merlin is an example of a poor upstart who had prospered to such a degree as to come to believe that a fanatical and pitiless attainment of power and wealth was man's only salvation on earth. Television, and the arts in general, were a mere business venture for him, profitable commodities. Rhydwen's contrasting belief is represented by the views of Stephen O'Neill, the company's drama producer: a television establishment should be even more critical of the quality of its output than the public itself in order to nurture character and integrity; its programmes should reflect a persistent and developing dedication, a diligence to the arts rather than to financial profiteering. The television industry is lampooned where it lacks human warmth. Rhydwen has always been highly critical of all institutions and individuals who lack the values that give life meaning — those short on the *geniality which strikes a chord in other people.*

GALLT Y GOFAL is based on the tragic life of an old acquaintance; a man who always had to lead an uphill struggle of woes and grief like the ones described by Lewis Morris in his poem of *hen benillion:*

Blinder ysbryd yw gofalon,
Dringo'r Allt sydd doriad calon,
Lle bo dyn â chalon feddal,
Duw, mor flin yw Gallt y Gofal.

(Anxieties weary the soul,
Climbing the Hill is heartbreaking,
To a kind-hearted man,
God, how difficult is the Hill of Tribulation.)

Job Cornog is a sensitive, passionate, depressed prone introvert victimized from birth, when his mother died, by a series of harsh misfortunes. He is always on the escape from one predicament to another, forever in search of lasting love and contentment, a satisfaction which persistently eludes him. After the sudden death of his young wife he stumbles into the army soon to find himself in the middle of the armageddon in France where he is wounded and forced to leave active service. After his return home he habitually tries to fill his life's void by debauchery until he comes to the state of utter surfeit from which he makes his final escape by means of suicide:

You always thought you were performing so skilfully, everybody falling about within a mile of your jokes, every Lisa and Betty like a midwife at your service, and nobody noticing your uncertain, servile, lonely, defenceless, guilty face behind your mask, persevering to search for someone to love, embrace and possess you, but — you didn't get nobody — nobody to adhere — nobody to stay.

Until you came to your last sweetheart, the Black Angel, behind the closed door of the garage . . . and laying your head down comfortably . . . and switching the engine on . . .

GALLT Y GOFAL has more than the eye meets in common with APOLO only that the similarity works from opposite poles. John Merlin, Apolo's despot is the inflicter of ruthlessness, corruption and strife; Job Cornog, on the other hand, is the recipient of life's merciless blows, but both characters are equally unhappy and sick at heart. The two novelettes meet in the same psychological truism: a life forlorn of genuine love is fated for unavoidable misery.

VI

In 1980 Rhydwen Williams was appointed editor of BARN the Welsh monthly periodical. He spent six years in the chair during which his chief aim, as he outlined in the editorial of the March 1984 edition, was to make BARN an accessible platform for Welsh writers and critics. His most significant and interesting editorials, from September 1981 to July 1986, express his concern on three main issues with a crucial interconnection, thereby forming a compact and a complete editorial vision.

The first was for the plight of the Welsh language. Here he speaks with admiration for the young campaigners, and often their families as well, who had to endure anguish and insult, frequently at the indifferent hands of their fellow-countrymen, in their struggle on behalf of their mother tongue:

Autumn 1981

A few months ago I wrote a sermon on a subject from the Psalms — 'And they bound their sacrifices to the altar'. The point of the simple homily was, whoever makes a sacrifice for a principle, ties other offerings to the altar of that principle. I am thinking of Wayne Williams and his young wife and his child.

Wayne cannot be true to his vision concerning Wales without tying them, his loved ones, to the altar's posts. It is irresponsible and unworthy to say that the fault is his, and that he knew the consequences. As we said about the Maze prisoners, agreeing with them or not, any human being who is willing to go to such extremes for his conviction deserves to be taken seriously, and every prejudicial reaction still keeps man and society deep in the bog of our uncivilized primitivism. We repeat that everyone who sacrifies for any conviction is obliged to bind other sacrifices to the altar.

I have been talking recently with some mothers whose children have committed a symbolical act for Wales, and I realized how each of these women was a sacrifice on behalf of our language and existence. The marks of the altar were on their foreheads and indication of the sacrifice in their eyes.

April 1982

It is an extremely sad day when the students of one of the colleges of Wales, children on home soil, have to form a society and start a campaign like this to guard their mother tongue and secure their own position in an establishment which is part of their entitlement. . . Of course, it is no surprise to hear people versed in nothing other than Bingo and an occasional authoritative lout of a policeman who talks as if a tap was lodged in his mouth not a tongue (at this moment in time) reviling the young who think and rationalize a nation's fate and their personal responsibility, but it is desperately sad when wise men and teachers and cultured people, given the trust of administering an inheritance amongst its inheritors, refuse to listen, ignore a plea, and turn one of the foremost defences of our language and culture and dignity as a nation into a barrack where vagrants call in for a bowl of broth and a bed for the night.

Rhydwen continues to underline the critical importance of the persistence of the campaign in the face of ill will and opposition from several Welsh bodies. These particular editorials have their own brand of attachment and wrath arising from dwelling in depth on the uniqueness of his endangered language and the value of its irreplaceable treasures:

55

July/August 1982

It is the Eisteddfod of our language and literature and traditions which makes our small nation very special in the world at the moment.

The President of the National Eisteddfod is not some minor chairman of a committee but perhaps the nearest Wales can come to a prime minister or president, and he should be greeted and welcomed so in every circle.

September 1983

. . . the activity of Cymdeithas yr Iaith on behalf of a Body to Develop Welsh Education must be seen as one of the most important issues in our life, indeed if not the most important of all!

. . . the Welsh language has a fierce battle in some territories which should be foremost in its defences, where its rights are refused under the excuse of disfavouring the English people and their language, if you ever heard such nonsense!

June 1984

Cymraeg is the golden key for a full relationship with family and nation, and the cultural education of that mother tongue is the right of every child. The sadness in Wales is that so many of our fellow-countrymen have been robbed of this all-important key, they now regard English as their mother tongue.

By realizing the ill feeling of many councillors in Wales towards the language and the rights of our children to their education and culture, it is not repugnant by many of us to swear with every vulgarity against such repulsiveness.

In his second issue, the editor broadens his concern from the difficulties facing his own culture to embrace

56

the threat imperilling the entire earth. The direct anger so apparent in the preceding quotations is replaced by a laughable sarcasm corresponding to the absurd nature of the object of its derision, the build up of nuclear weapons in the West:

September 1981

. . . it is not only the future of the small chapels of Wales or our periodicals, language and welfare that are at stake, but the entire planet here and now.

December/January 1983-4

Of every Christmas since the birth of Christ (and, certainly, within living memory), this is the saddest in the history of the human race. In the twentieth century A.D., and after all the preaching, worshipping and devotion to facilitate Christian values, Wales and every country around her received the most accursed gift ever devised.

An aeroplane arrived from America on Monday morning, November 14, 1983 as punctual and stealthy as Santa Claus to present that which is a thousand times more valuable than gold, frankincense and myrrh in the eyes of the political wise men of the modern world, a splendid bomb which has a hundred times more power than the comparative toy which shattered Hiroshima.

April 1985

Today, no country pretends to be more Christian than America. She sends her evangelists on costly campaigns over the world to announce the full Gospel to make the sinners of Wales, England, Ireland and Scotland, and even materialistic Marxists and the most ardent of the Russian KGB repent, and her aged president is so pious, prayerful and Biblical that he cannot end an interview or speech without adding, 'Gad bless America!'

But the blessing of the Infinite God is not worth a button, in spite of that, nor the security of his wounded Christ, to a single soul whose parliament is not spending billions on new missiles to expand the boundaries of the next armageddon to the very extremities of space. And that is not sufficient either; a portion of the bombs must be kept on our threshold. It is of no importance if we are blown to eternity and tomorrow's citizens murdered in the womb, so far as to make sure that the enemy goes the same way.

Thirdly, Rhydwen offers a religious remedy for both of the above political maladies — the traditions and teachings of the Christian faith. Here, he even rebukes the younger generation in their total lack of adherence and loyalty to this fundamental aspect of Welsh life. His tone is one of earnest conviction that only Christianity can wholly meet the gravity of the Welsh nation's predicament as well as soothe the volatile disposition of modern man:

September 1981

Some of us lament that it looks as if there is no future for Welsh chapels, a natural response after serving them for nearly forty years. It is regrettable to see many of the younger generation, zealous on behalf of the language and the noblest rights of the nation, but without allegiance to what our forefathers called 'The Cause', nor interest in it, without the slightest recognition that it is only this Christianity which is accountable that we have a language at present to worry about and possessions and priveleges to safeguard. It appears to some of us quite impossible to defend the Welsh language and our rights and values as a nation in a materialistic, infidel, Christless Wales, and by this we do not imply for a second that the only alternative is an old-fashioned little country, narrow in its ideas, conservative in its ways and reeking of camphor and prejudices. We maintain that the Welsh chapels at their best stood chiefly for the dominion of Christ over the individual and nation, a vision which has dimmed in front of

58

the eyes of many of us from time to time, but it is difficult to see how 'the well can be kept free of dirt' and 'the vineyard which was given' to us, 'for our children and children's children' without acknowledging that fact in repentance and faith and devotion.

Autumn 1982

. . . without the Christian Church, whatever its form and condition, the Wales which the majority of us romanticize about and the minority sacrifice and suffer for, will be a country without romance to offer as an inspiration to anyone nor glory deserving the sacrifice of a single brave soul.

December 1985

Any belief or creed which tames and appeases our nature is more than valuable. Any philosophy or gospel which can make-selfish and unmanageable creatures like small children is at the top of the list of mankind's deepest needs.

VII

In 1981, when he was sixty-five, Rhydwen Williams was taken seriously ill with a seizure which paralysed his left side. His fight to regain health is a story of dogged determination, and the way in which he persevered to edit BARN and continue with his creative work, during his illness, an example of unrelenting courage. The following testimony appeared in the column 'Sylwadau'r Mis' (*Remarks of the Month*) of the February 1982 edition of BARN *I have never seen from anyone such a spiritual, mental and physical effort as Rhydwen Williams's endeavour.*

True to his nature, very soon he was back hard at it editing a volume of essays in honour of Kate Roberts which appeared in 1983. The following year he published GORWELION and DEI GRATIA, a book which is an expression of his gleeful gratitude for a recovery of health. Its series of religious poems is of special significance because they truly revel in announcing the unbelievable paradoxical fact that the meek and unpretentious Christ of the Incarnation is so overwhelmingly more powerful than the mighty temporal powers of earth, superior to philosophical and scientific knowledge and far more exalted than the pomp of learning:

Ffarwel, fawrion ymerodrol ac offeiriaid ffôl,
rhyw oedi yng nghysgod y Mab bychan fydd mwyach eich rhôl!

mae symlrwydd yr Aer yn chwilfriwio hen gaer ein geiriau,
a gwyleidd-dra'r Baban yn drech nag ymffrost prifysgolion.

   (Farewell, imperial powers and foolish priests,
   your role evermore to tarry in the shadow of Mary's Son!

the Heir's simplicity shatters the old fortress of our words,
and the Babe's humility is stronger than the prestige of
universities.)

In his zest the poet's expression of the struggle which the Kingdom of Love had to endure in order to triumph over Man's conniving establishments shows originality. He maintains that the sharpest grief of Mary was not the actual death of her Son, but having to witness the priests and politicians gaining the upper hand on His young Kingdom; and, therefore the great joy of the Resurrection for her was not conquering Death, as such, but victory over the forces which threatened the dominion of His teachings. In the poem 'Dweud' (*Uttering*) Rhydwen realizes that Christ's unobtrusive, yet infallible manner of working is poles apart from Man's impatient and vociferous expectations which always demand immediate results and visible proof. 'Panis Angelicus', the collection's most concise and effective poem — some of the others do suffer at times from incompactness and verbosity — testifies directly and characteristically with feeling to the final victory of faith over the chill of despair in man's soul:

Heb boeni mwyach
ai disgyn o'r nef a wnaeth
neu chwarae ar draws y dychymyg,
y mae'r blas ar yr hen wefusau hyn
yn eu hebrwng, bererinion,
fel ar ddechrau'r daith,
i ben draw'r siwrnai.

(Not worrying henceforth
whether it descended from heaven
or played across the imagination,
the taste on these old lips

accompanies them, the pilgrims,
as at the beginning
to the journey's end.)

In 1986 YS GWN I A CHERDDI ERAILL *(I Wonder and Other Poems)* appeared. Its most interesting theme is its sensitive portrayals of the innocent and harmless in the face of life's inevitable destructive and tyrannical forces. This is mostly represented by a number of symbolical animal poems. For instance, the instinctive fear of the spider stands for the dread of the vulnerable everywhere, and the sight of a bright fish wriggling on a hook for the annihilation of beauty in general. The nightingale is regarded as superior to the proud and lordly eagle on account of the prowess of its song. The aspirations of the Creator were satisfied with the form and nature bestowed on a creature like the crab, but man's reaction to the crustacean was to boil it alive in order to satisfy his gastronomic craving.

The theme is also symbolized by two substantial political poems. In 'Cusan' *(Kiss)* the imprisonment of Nelson Mandela is bitingly criticized and his separation from his family tenderly worded. A relentless mood of shame diffuses through its gentility since it was inspired by the reading of Mandela's letters on the day the Welsh rugby team returned from South Africa:

Tithau, heb ddim ar d'elw ond y wisg amdanat
ac angerdd y cusan a wesgi ar wydr y gwahanfur . . .

Ond be' fedrwn ni ei wneud drosot, ni Gymry diofidiau,
na feddwn y fath sêl dros linach na thraddodiad na dim,
dim ond hwrli-bwrli'r bêl hirgron, yr unig ddewrder a
*   wyddom?*
Nelson Mandela, maddau i ni am ddifyrru'r gweilch a'th
*   gondemniodd gyhyd!*

(You, with nothing except your garment
and the passion of a kiss pressed on the separating glass . . .

But what can we do for you, we the carefree Welsh,
who have no such zeal for race or tradition at all,
only the hurly-burly of a rugby ball, the only courage we
        know?
Nelson Mandela, forgive us entertaining the ruffians who
        condemned you so long!)

The other poem exemplifies the unavoidable clash between life's two major energies by investigating the inner issues of a confrontation between an armed American soldier on guard outside a nuclear arsenal and a young pregnant Welsh protester:

Saif ef dros genedl fawr
na oddef yn enw'r Ffydd feiddgarwch niwcliar neb
nac ystyfnigrwydd na nonsens chwaith,
crancod y Kremlin neu'r groten o'r hen gwm.

Saif hi dros hyn:
yr hawl i fod yn ifanc
a'r hawl i farw'n hen;
yr hawl i garu rhywun
a'r hawl i greu o'r groth;
yr hawl i fyd heb fom —
hyn oll heb ofyn ffafr
a heb ferthyrdod chwaith.

(He stands for a big nation
that in Faith's name will not tolerate anybody's nuclear
        threat
or stubborness or nonsense either,
be they cranks from the Kremlin or the girl from the old
        valley.

She stands for this:
the right to be young
and the right to die old;
the right to love someone
and the right to create in the womb;
to live without fears
and a world with no bomb-scare —
all this without begging favour
and without martyrdom either.)

Furthermore, the poem 'Gwawr' *(Dawn)* insists that *the shameless hooters of our worthy civilization* always shatter the beauty of dawn to reground us in our drab fatigued existence. According to 'Nadolig' *(Christmas)* the new entertaining human trinities of our age have ousted the Holy Trinity, and the journey to Bethlehem pales insignificantly in comparison with our zooming visits to distant planets. In all this, the poet does not retreat from directly confronting the basic cause of our entire tribulations and suffering; unswervingly, he traces it back to its ancient root — the original transgression in Eden.

In his next three books, PEDWARAWD, 1986 *(Quartet)*; AMSER I WYLO, 1986 *(A Time to Weep)*; and RHONDDA POEMS, 1987, Rhydwen returns once more to his valley.

The first, PEDWARAWD a series of four lengthy poems, reminiscent of Eliot's FOUR QUARTETS, traces the poet's spiritual journey from perplexity and emptiness to certitude and faith, each progression connected with a special place of importance in his life. In the first, 'Senghennydd', the scene of the catastrophic pit disaster in 1913 is one of darkness. Life seems an empty existence on a senseless planet. The fate of the colliers, men and children alike, is starkly described and related in certain phases to various tragic counterparts in Welsh literature: the early morning journey of the colliers to work, their descent to the pit and their toil underground are illustrated in the manner which Aneirin used in his sixth- century heroic poem 'Y Gododdin' to picture the eager march of the three-hundred Briton warriors from Edinburgh to be slaughtered on Catterick field; a mother's grief is worded on the agonizing style of Lewys Glyn Cothi's lament after his five-year old son, Siôn; a tribute to a dead pit horse is ironically paid on the pattern of the luxurious cywydd of Tudur Aled to the splendid steed he asked Dafydd ab Owain, the abbot of Aberconwy in the sixteenth century, to bestow as a gift upon Lewis ap Madog of Llaneurgain in Flintshire. An attitude of utter bafflement before ghastly incomprehensible circumstances permeates the whole *pryddest* leading to bitterness, isolation and alienation from faith:

> *Ond y mae dyfnder i ing*
> *sy'n ddyfnach na'r boen sy'n treiddio*
> *i'r cnawd; gwewyr a bair brotest*
> *yn erbyn dyn a Duw, gan erfyn am*
> *ymwared, solas a chymwynas, mwy;*
> *awr pan adewir dyn i'w dynged;*
> *y tywyllwch a all lenwi'r enaid*
> *i brofi'r Hollbresennol yn absennol . . .*
> *chwerwder a etyl ynom ras a chariad!*

> *Ystyr ni bydd i'w stori*
> *a'u hangeuau a anghofir*
> *mor wir â'r llanw ymerodrol*
> *a ylch ymaith olion manion y môr*
> *a'u miri, heb adael undim ar ôl.*

(But there is a depth to agony
deeper than the pain which penetrates
the flesh; an anguish causing protest
against man and God, pleading
for deliverance, solace and favour, more;
an hour when a man is left to his fate;
the darkness which can fill the soul
to prove the absence of the Allpresent . . .
a bitterness which impedes within us grace and love!

Their story will be meaningless
and their deaths forgotten
as sure as the imperial tide
which washes away the triflings of the sea
and their frolick, leaving nothing behind.)

The second part, 'Tynybedw', dwells nostalgically on the fleeting nature of life's happy seasons in time's course. We catch an echo of 'East Coker' here in the depiction of each generation passing by on its march towards oblivion:

A dylifa'r dyrfa heibio
tua glan yr afon,
mamau a thadau a hen gewri
ynghyd â bechgyn a merched bach
a'r gwŷr ieuainc hynny a drengodd
fel y dail a lithra'n dawel ymaith
ac a gwymp ar lawr y goedwig
ym mrathiad cynta'r hydref. . .

(And the throng flows past
towards the riverside,
mothers and fathers and old giants
together with boys and little girls
and the youths who perished
like the leaves slip quietly away
and fall on the forest's floor

in the first stab of autumn . . .)

The inevitability of old age is shown by a number of portraits of elderly characters, each one with his different experience, response and outlook, but all in line for the same fate. People, like the beasts and plants, are made of clay, and Mother Nature, in all her abundance and haphazardness, the sole director of life:

— *Di, Natur, ein mam, ein chwaer, ein meistres a beraist i'r*
Assisi ddawnsio wrth weld adar y to, eraill i wallgofi wrth
wrando'r eos yn canu, a'r ap Gwilym i ffoli ar ferch, pan
anadla'r crogwr ar ein trefi a'n pentrefi, trugarha!

(— *You, Nature, our mother, our sister, our mistress, who*
       caused
the Assisi to rejoice on seeing the sparrows, others to ecstasy
listening to the nightingale, and ap Gwilym to dote on a girl,
       when
the hangman breathes on our towns and villages, take pity!)

Eliot's influence, however, is more discernible in the third poem, 'Mynydd Lliw'. Here a fleeting conception, a momentary revelation of God is caught amongst the humdrum hours of existence similar to the manner by which the *heart of light, the still point of the turning world* is glimpsed through *the moment in the rose-garden* in 'Burnt Norton', and *the point of intersection of the timeless with time* in 'Dry Salvages':

> *Cerddwch y llwybr gwlithog*
> *dan fwâu rhosynnog yr ardd,*
> *heibio'r goeden feichiog yn y berllan fach,*
> *yno, yn anadl y blodau, y mae'r Presenoldeb*
> *yn ymgomio â ni*
> *mor reial â'r siwrne gynt i Emaus . . .*

(Walk the dewy path
beneath the garden's rosy arches,
past the laden tree in the small orchard,
there, in the flower's breath, the Presence
is conversing with us
as real as on the old journey to Emaus . . .)

He is viewed as the Allpresent who can be felt as readily amongst the screech of factories as in the midst of leaves, rivers and breezes. He is nearer than the artery in our throats, the mysterious act and actor on the stage of mortality. Finally, the mysticism is abandoned and his identity and abode acknowledged and named in terms of Isaiah's vision: He is the Almighty who sits on the elevated throne surrounded by the seraphim.

The last part, 'Pwll y Twr', develops this theme to its furthermost orthodox aspect. The Last Supper and Christ's strange mission on earth are convincingly embraced:

Breuddwyd am bŵer oedd hyn;
y grym a ddaw trwy fod yn ddirym neu'n ddof;
nid gorfodi daioni ar neb;
cariad sy'n derbyn croes,
dioddefaint sy'n fraint hyfryd,
a'r duw yntau sy'n derbyn ei ddistrywio
am y gŵyr mai ei gariad
yw maen a chonglfaen hyn o fyd.

(This was a dream about power
the power which comes by being submissive or meek;
not inflicting virtue on anyone;
a love which bears a cross,
a suffering which is a glorious privilege,
and the god who is willing to be destroyed
since he knows love
is the corner stone of the world.)

68

The risen Christ filled the emptiness of His grieving disciples and His message was carried, from then on, to all times to perpetuate Love and create that which was *a richness in the invisible* from the beginning. Since *the mystery is hidden in every creation*, and all of nature unable to express it comprehensibly, the convinced testifiers and witnesses of the centuries are our only encouragers and inspiration *to venture unto the threshold of the eternal:*

> *Mentrwn y mynydd*
> *yn ddistaw yn y bore bach*
> *pan fo'r gwlith*
> *yn cusanu'r copâu;*
> *ni a welwn yn gloywi'r glaswellt*
> *ôl eu traed,*
> *y rhai addfwyn*
> *a'r pur o galon,*
> *mor brydferth ar y bryniau*
> *â'r mireinder a edy'r Dwylo*
> *ar esgyll y pili-pala.*

> *(Let us risk the mountain*
> *quietly at dawn*
> *when the dew*
> *kisses the peaks;*
> *we shall see their footsteps*
> *glistening the grass,*
> *the gentle ones*
> *and the pure ones*
> *and the pure of heart,*
> *so fair on the hills*
> *as the beauty which the Hands embroider*
> *on the butterfly's wings.)*

AMSER I WYLO (*A Time to Weep*) which won the Daniel Owen Memorial Prize is an interesting contemporary novel owing to its unusual plot — a simple clear-cut four-phased series of character sketches, reports and documentary evidence. And here such an approach is extremely effective, central in the success of the composition, mainly because the nature of its subject — the Senghennydd disaster of 1913 — lent itself creatively and morally to this kind of plan and vision.

Firstly, an ironic cross-section of life in the valley is drawn through affectionate outlines of twenty-one colliers, men of different temperaments and backgrounds, often pictured on the eve of the explosion in their various natural whereabouts. Secondly, they are described on their way to work the following morning, surrounded by their industrial history and the domineering influence of Lord Merthyr. Thirdly, a selection of extracts from newspaper reports is used to reveal the carnage itself. Fourthly, the lonely grief-torn bereaved ones are concisely portrayed, and then the tedious enquiry, mainly centred on one man, Edward Shaw, the pit manager, is carefully traced, in which, finally, the entire blame for the death of 440 men was laid on him with a fine of £24, and the owner totally exempted. A year later the catastrophe is shown to be in the process of being forgotten in the general bustle at the start of the First World War.

AMSER I WYLO is a poet's novel with a traditional plot woven around a typical heroic tragedy, and infused with a disturbing matter-of-fact contemporary spirit. Its marked strength arises out of this duality: the ironic contrast between the warm neighbourly atmosphere of the first two sections and the abrupt official tone of the last two, the conflicting source of its sympathy and remorseful scorn.

70

RHONDDA POEMS, is a collection of English verse, a combination of translations from the Welsh and original work, written to communicate with those people of the poet's generation who unfortunately are unable to speak Welsh as a result of the historic break up which the Rhondda society experienced. This intention imbued the poems with a flavour all of their own in the sense that the English adopted makes a creative and stimulating use of Welsh rhythms and idioms. The volume generated suffcient local interest and enthusiasm to be published with the support of Mr Alan Evans of Gwalia Inns Ltd., Hirwaun. The reasons given by the author in the foreword for its creation are so heavily laden with meaning that they deserve to be fully quoted:

I never had to learn my mother's tongue as such, it came to me with my mother's milk, and I'm not sure what favours the English language can do for my poems — liberating perchance some suppressed part of my personality, albeit chancing a little vulgarity? What I do know is that many of my kin and generation for different reasons have been denied the mother-tongue and have more than once during the years — like Christopher Logue once in the Rotterdam Poetry Festival asked, 'Translation, please, share your poetry with us!' I've always felt unhappy at being unable to oblige, but it's an inevitability unless we want the English language to take over the world. Alas, human life and civilization would become as boring as rainbows of one colour!

RHONDDA POEMS is a most unusual kind of Anglo-Welsh poetry in that it has a background, subject matter, concern, overtones and purpose entirely particular to itself:

> *Who was to know*
> *that to disturb the wildflower,*
> *the intimate curlew and the native kite,*
> *the curious squirrel — domiciled since Eden —*

71

and the little lambs that snowflaked the fields,
would eventually lead to:
    fire and water along dicey seams,
    dust on the clothes-line and dust in the lungs,
    the suicide on the landing and the scandal in the choir,
    the piano in the parlour and the medals on the
          mantlepiece,
    the picture on the sideboard and the cap-and-gown in the
          wardrobe,
    the baby in the cot and the rose in the garden,
    the silence in the bandroom and the noise in the bar,
    the hands on the organ and the preacher in the pulpit,
    the sheep in the ash-bucket and the stranger in the shop,
    the names on the cenotaph and the children in the park . . .
and an old language
on an old man's lips
struggling to converse
with a new generation?

VIII

In LIWSI REGINA, which appeared in 1988, Rhydwen Williams progressed as a novelist by carving a new trail for himself far out from the well-beaten path through the iron and coal producing valleys of his own times into the fresh territory of another age, and that for the first time in a substantial Welsh composition, to trace the life story of Lucy Walter, a member of Roch Castle's gentry in Pembrokeshire, during and after the English Civil War. Here, also, he concentrated on producing a much smoother narrative than that of his earlier novels, abandoning to a greater degree, albeit not altogether, his frequent tendency to interrupt the natural growth of a story with chunks of factual material. But even in this novel there are examples where the historian or indeed his experience in television, insisted on getting the better of the novelist, and in such places the historical facts stand out too prominently without sufficient narrative density to cover their gaunt, abrupt framework. But much more often, they have been organically woven into a rich fabric of persistent story-telling. The art of pure narrative, descriptive ingenuity and conflicting imagination, the power and sensitivity of a many-faceted style, is very much in the forefront in LIWSI REGINA with enriching and effective results. It enables the reader to associate himself strongly with the atmosphere of everyday life in the seventeenth century, and to feel the corrupt and oppressive nature of the politics of the period, especially the disruptive manner by which inaccessible and hidden decisions perpetrated by conspirators affected unsuspecting individuals. In this, Lucy's era is not so different from our own.

But there is a deeper significance to the work than narrative dexterity. LIWSI REGINA is a symbolic novel. Lucy's tragic life as the mistress of Charles II amongst the English ruling class and royal family of the day is seen as a symbol of Wales's disgrace under a foreign power. Wales degenerates into a whore in order to satisfy the lascivious demands of her English conquerors, a line of thought exploited earlier by Gwenallt in his sonnet 'Cymru' in YSGUBAU'R AWEN (*Sheaves of Inspiration*), 1938, where he deplores the nation's fall from her elevated position to a *dirty prostitute with a servile voice*. Rhydwen himself used a somewhat similar symbolism in his poem 'Alcestis'. It will be remembered that Admetos, the king of Pherai in Greek mythology, managed to win the fair Alcestis as his wife by an exhibition of might — driving a chariot drawn by a wild boar and a lion around the racing track at Iolchos. England is the Admetos of the poem, whereas Alcestis is Wales, the gentle maiden whom the imperial sovereign lustfully desires in order to satisfy his greed.

It is stipulated that Wales is England's dogsbody and that her inhabitants are bought serfs. This concept is an obvious feature of the novel; the full meaning of the following words discharged by the frustrated Lucy on one occasion at her royal lover could not be more forthright:

The only way you can rid yourselves from guilt is to make a scapegoat of others, as you did to us Welsh. Making the royal lineage divine and assuming to be an elected nation, thinking my people nothing more than churls fit to feed pigs or a prey for your pagan wars.

74

An obvious autobiographical element also winds through the novel. The first point to take note of in connection with this is the long period which Lucy had to spend in exile. She was uprooted from her home near St. Brides Bay at a green age. In this she is similar to her portrayer. We have amply felt by now the continuous significance of this trauma of transference throughout Rhydwen's work. And it is precisely this anxiety which makes it so relevant to the present critical situation of the nation. Lucy's tragic exile could be interpreted as an extension of the author's uneasy experiences in similar circumstances. Therefore, although LIWSI REGINA is different in expression and content from the other novels, its passions and fundamental meaning spring from exactly the same agonizing Welsh source.

There is also an autobiographical slant to the religious aspects of the novel. One of its strongest chapters is that in which Lucy challenges Cromwell and his parliamentarians on the issue of their self-righteous faith. It glows with feeling as the girl argues defiantly on behalf of an inquisitive approach and virtuous common sense in religious matters in the presence of the inflexible single-minded Puritans. Their unyielding response to Lucy's reasoning reminds us of the hard attitude Rhydwen once faced regarding his militant humanitarian views in student days. His criticism of religious extremism may be seen in the picture drawn of the complete insanity which overwhelms William Walter, Lucy's father, after his conversion by the fiery Puritan, Vavasor Powell. Betsan's verdict, one of William's lovers, on his condition concisely represents the author's strong view on the whole matter: *All well and good to have religion in the heart, but when it heats the head ... Oh, it's bad then.* He might very well have inherited this faculty of the importance of keeping clarity of mind and a sane intellect in connection with religious affairs from his mother and Uncle Siôn, since both depended on the guidance of sound, well-developed reasoning powers throughout their spiritual journey.

Critics, sometimes, are inclined to condemn the historical novelist who has the tendency not to pay sufficient attention to factual exactness and precise details. They see this as unfaithfulness to the ethos of the particular age he is portraying. LIWSI REGINA has already received such a critique. And yet, although it is wise for a novelist to show reverence for factual truth, so far as possible, his first allegiance is to the truth and integrity of his own art. In other words, he has an artistic right to make his historical characters represent his own personal view of life although they might not be altogether suitable in every detail for such an interpretation. Indeed, more than one of our leading critics and scholars have articulately testified in favour of this literary philosophy. To quote one example: Professor R. Geraint Gruffydd shows approvingly in 'Hanes rhyw Gymro' (*A History of some Welshman*), a study in JOHN GWILYM JONES, CYFROL DEYRNGED (*A Tributary Volume*) that the playwright's portrait of Morgan Llwyd is quite different from that of the historian:

As we were distinctly reminded by Robert Williams Parry, there is a difference between the dramatist's truth and the historian's truth. Mr Jones' purpose was not to interpret the historical Morgan Llwyd in HANES RHYW GYMRO *but to imply a definite vision on life in the terms of Morgan Llwyd's life history — and it is the vision that is important, not the history.*

Rhydwen certainly adopted that policy. He created his own Lucy. According to historians, the explicit evidence on the complete life course of the Walter family is scanty. There is no knowledge of Lucy's parents after the termination of their long drawn out divorce case, from 1641 to 1647, other than dates of their deaths — William Walter died in 1650 and Elizabeth Walter in 1652. Much more is known about her relations with Charles Stuart and his mother, Henrietta Maria. But again there seems to be no certainty regarding her death. Sir J. F. Rees's remark on the matter in 'The Parents of Lucy Walter' in STUDIES IN WELSH HISTORY is nebulous: *Lucy is said to have died in poverty in 1658.* And there is certainly no evidence for the political patriotic ardour attributed to Lucy in the novel. Professor David Williams like Professor A. H. Dodd maintains that such a sentiment was not one of the features of the majority of Welsh gentry in the seventeenth century. Lucy's fundamental characteristics are the creations of the author's own ideas and imagination rather than a paraphrase of historical facts. In her, he discovered a character with whom he could readily identify and project on to his personal afflictions and beliefs.

To account for ancestry, territory and achievements only would be to fail lamentably short of the mark in assessing Rhydwen Williams, without referring to the mainspring of his whole career — his marriage to Margaret, daughter of Thomas and Catherine Davies of Porth, Rhondda, and the home established wherever life has led them, displaying proudly among its treasures the sculpture, paintings and drawings of an artist-son, Huw Rhydwen.

We both arrived at a point in life, he acknowledges, *where a compulsion to return to the valleys of our origin proved irresistible. Weary of cities and towns, we yearned for hills that embraced our upbringing, and the sturdy walls that housed the people to whom we belonged.* Such a dream came true for them twenty-years ago.

The lady of the house presides over what is unmistakably the home of a poet. Walls and shelves cater for past awards discreetly. A life-time's devotion to books is shelved from the hallway to the 'gazebo' at the furthermost point of the garden. The 'study' is snug — *a well-feathered nest made for an early bird.* Next to it, the bard favours the 'kitchen' — *where a good cook leaves aromas of splendid fare as agreeable as incense to a papist.* Two solid desks, a word processor, phone, reams of paper and a bed alongside — *make life easier for my slightly battered, yet unbeaten body.*

Up with the dawn, Rhydwen Williams's prolific diligence continues . . .

A Selected Bibliography

RHYDWEN WILLIAMS

Poetry

CERDDI CADWGAN, Swansea, Gwasg Cadwgan, 1953 (with D. R. Griffiths, Pennar Davies, Gareth Alban Davies and J. Gwyn Griffiths).
AR Y CYD, Bala, Gwasg y March Gwyn, 1962 (with Huw T. Edwards, Mathonwy Hughes and Gwilym R. Jones).
BARDDONIATH RHYDWEN WILLIAMS, Llandybïe, Christopher Davies, 1965.
Y FFYNHONNAU A CHERDDI ERAILL, Llandybïe, Christopher Davies, 1970.
Y CHWYLDRO GWYRDD, Llandybïe, Christopher Davies, 1972.
YSTLUMOD, Swansea, Christopher Davies, 1975.
DEI GRATIA, Cyhoeddiadau Barddas, 1984.
YS GWYN I A CHERDDI ERAILL, Cyhoeddiadau Barddas, 1986.
PEDWARAWD, Cyhoeddiadau Barddas, 1986.
RHONDDA POEMS, Swansea, Christopher Davies, 1987.

Novels

CWM HIRAETH: Y BRIODAS, Llandybïe, Christopher Davies, 1969.
CWM HIRAETH: Y SIÔL WEN, Llandybïe, Christopher Davies, 1970.

ADAR Y GWANWYN, Llandybïe, Christopher Davies, 1972.

BREUDDWYDD RHONABWY JONES, Llandybïe, Christopher Davies, 1972.

CWM HIRAETH: DYDDIAU DYN, Llandybïe, Christopher Davies, 1973.

THE ANGRY VINEYARD, Swansea, Christopher Davies, 1975.

APOLO, Swansea, Christopher Davies, 1975.

GALLT Y GOFAL, Swansea, Christopher Davies, 1979.

AMSER I WYLO: SENGHENNYDD 1913, Swansea, Christopher Davies, 1986.

LIWSI REGINA, Swansea, Christopher Davies, 1988.

Miscellaneous

KATE ROBERTS: EI MEDDWL A'I GWAITH, Christopher Davies, 1983 (editor).

GORWELION, Llandybïe, Christopher Davies, 1984 - (autobiography).

Criticism of Rhydwen Williams

Jones, R. M. : 'Yr Amharch Rhydwen Williams', HANES LLENYDDIAETH GYMRAEG 1936-1972, Llandybïe, Christopher Davies, 1975.

Llwyd, Alan: 'Chwech o Feirdd', BARDDONIAETH Y CHWEDEGAU: ASTUDIAETH LENYDDOL-HANESYDDOL, Cyhoeddiadau Barddas, 1986.

Acknowledgements

I should like to express sincere thanks to the following:

Y Prifardd Rhydwen Williams for countless talks and permission to quote freely from his books; *y Prifardd* Alan Llwyd for casting an eye over the manuscript; Dr R. Brinley Jones for the benefit of his editorial thoroughness; Mr Ned Thomas, Director of the University of Wales Press, for his sensitive interest in the work; the Welsh Arts Council for the commission to write.

The Author

Donald Evans was born on Banc Siôn Cwilt, Ceredigion, in 1940. He was educated at Aberaeron Secondary School and the University College of Wales, Aberystwyth where he gained an honours degree in Welsh. He taught Welsh at Ardwyn Grammar School, Aberystwyth and Penglais Comprehensive School, Aberystwyth. He won both the Crown and the Chair at the Wrexham National Eisteddfod, 1977 and repeated the same feat at the Dyffryn Lliw Eisteddfod, 1981. He has also won three Welsh Arts Council Poetry Prizes and the Griffith John Williams Memorial Prize for his latest volume of poetry, IASAU. He is the author of ten poetry volumes, editor of Y FLODEUGERDD O GYWYDDAU, and a past Poetry Editor of BARN.

Designed by Jeff Clements
Typeset by BP Integraphics Ltd, Bath, in
Palatino 11pt on 13 pt and printed in Great Britain by
Qualitex Printing Limited, Cardiff, 1991.

© University of Wales, 1991

British Library Cataloguing in Publication Data

Evans, Donald, 1940–
    Rhydwen Williams. (Writers of Wales series)
    I. Title   II. Series
    891.6632

    ISBN 0–7083–1131–8

The publishers wish to acknowledge
the financial assistance of the
Welsh Arts Council towards the cost
of producing this volume

All rights reserved. No part of this book may be
reproduced, stored in a retrieval system or
transmitted, in any form or by any means, electronic,
mechanical, photocopying, recording or otherwise,
without clearance from the University of Wales Press,
6 Gwennyth Street, Cardiff, CF2 4YD.